JOHN DEERE

Stonescaping Made Simple

Bring the Beauty of Stone Into Your Yard

Kristen Hampshire
& David Griffin

Creative Publishing
international

MINNEAPOLIS, MINNESOTA
www.creativepub.com

Creative Publishing international

Copyright © 2009
Creative Publishing international, Inc.
400 First Avenue North, Suite 300
Minneapolis, Minnesota 55401
1-800-328-3895
www.creativepub.com
All rights reserved

Printed in Singapore
10 9 8 7 6 5 4 3 2 1

Due to differing conditions, materials, and skill levels, the publisher and various manufacturers disclaim any liability for unsatisfactory results or injury due to improper use of tools, materials, or information in this publication.

Library of Congress Cataloging-in-Publication Data

Stonescaping made simple: bring the beauty of stone into your backyard.
        p. cm.
    "John Deere."
    Includes index.
    Summary: "Features information on basic tools and techniques for designing with stone. Includes several complete projects shown with step-by-step how-to photos"—Provided by publisher.
    ISBN-13: 978-1-58923-442-0 (soft cover)
    ISBN-10: 1-58923-442-1 (soft cover)
    1. Stone in landscape gardening. 2. Landscape construction.
3. Stonemasonry. I. Deere & Company. II. Title.

    SB475.5.S77 2009
    693'.1--dc22

2008045812

President/CEO: Ken Fund
VP for Sales & Marketing: Kevin Hamric

Publisher: Bryan Trandem
Managing Editor: Tracy Stanley
Senior Editor: Mark Johanson
Editor: Jennifer Gehlhar
Authors: Kristen Hampshire, David Griffin

Creative Director: Michele Lanci-Altomare
Senior Design Managers: Jon Simpson, Brad Springer
Design Manager: James Kegley

Lead Photographer: Steve Galvin
Photo Coordinator: Joanne Wawra
Shop Manager: Bryan McLain
Shop Assistant: Cesar Fernandez Rodriguez

Production Managers: Linda Halls, Laura Hokkanen

Cover Design: Heather Parlato
Page Layout Artist: Heather Parlato
Photographer: Joel Schnell
Shop Help: Charlie Boldt

Contents

Introduction

In many ways, stones are the bones of the earth. Sturdy and permanent, natural stone infuses history into a landscape, offering even a brand-new garden a sense of permanence and longevity—as if it had always been there. Consider the centuries-old cobble paths and brick walkways that meander unevenly through the historic towns of New England; or, imagine the rich Irish countryside and how it is both divided and beautified by its 250,000 miles of stone wall. From Stonehenge to the Great Wall of China to the Grand Canyon and Mount Rushmore, natural stone defines our world and our heritage in a unique and lovely way.

Stone in its many forms is a tangible, useful material that has a place in our own backyards. This is even more true today, with the array of increasingly convincing manufactured pavers that are tumbled and treated to resemble the "real thing." These materials are highly accessible and affordable. The color selection, textures, cuts, and paver sizes available will cater to any project you can dream up for your landscape. In this book, we'll provide you with the groundwork to execute a collection of projects that utilize natural stone and paver products.

THIS STACKED STONE WALL provides the framework for an outdoor kitchen. It combines natural and cast stones.

If you think about it, stone is the ultimate organic hardscaping material. Hardscape refers to masonry, wood, plastic, fiber—anything not living, blooming, and demanding of water or attention. Unlike plantings, stonescape is a permanent treatment for the landscape that frees busy homeowners from time-consuming maintenance activities.

Durability and longevity are hallmarks of a stonescaped area. Unlike a wood deck that requires regular cleaning and staining but will eventually rot or wear out, a patio of natural sandstone flags or cast concrete pavers requires little to no maintenance and will last as long as you care to keep it. In most cases, natural stone actually looks better once it ages.

Due to the high volume of foot traffic and stress we inflict upon our outdoor spaces, the stronger the materials we use in these areas the better. Natural and manufactured stone products are practical for retaining walls, walkways, and steps. Stonescape will also prevent erosion, punctuate a garden, create walls, separate outdoor rooms, guide foot traffic, and set the tone for your landscape design. Best of all, stone is the original maintenance-free building material—no weeding, mowing, or watering.

By incorporating stonescape and rock accents into your yard, you include a mineral element that adds a sense of balance. Stone doesn't look forced; it harmonizes with plants, ponds, and other features. When used judiciously with an eye toward proportion and scale, stone can complement its surroundings to the point of being virtually unnoticeable. It blends. On the other hand, stone makes a bold statement when treated as a centerpiece in a design. Interesting boulders serve as focal points. Rocks garnish water features, border flower beds, or nestle into gardens to add interest to plants such as sedum, creeping thyme, and moss. Stone's versatility opens up a wealth of creative possibilities.

There are many additional reasons why stone and paver look-alikes are in high demand. Perhaps the regenerated interest in the material is a reaction against yesterday's monolithic surfaces. While poured concrete and blacktop have certain advantages, they are more prone to cracking, buckling, and heaving; eventually allowing roots and weeds to spoil their surfaces and degrade their structural integrity. Stone doesn't suffer the same destruction with time. Pieced together like a puzzle, stonescape has more "give." Also, as we embrace more natural products and have a desire to work with the land, rather than just working it, stone is an ideal material. Or, it may simply be a matter of economics, as current global economic forces and increasing interest have made stone a more affordable option in many regions. Whichever reason matters most for you, now is the time to begin to build your stonescaping skills. *John Deere: Stonescaping Made Simple* is just the tool you need to do it.

BOULDERS STRATEGICALLY PLACED to retain a flower bed do double-duty in the landscape as both structural brace and visually pleasing accent.

Stonescape Design

Stone is a natural landscaping material that's at home in any yard or garden. Elegant and graceful, natural stone weathers well and in many cases actually improves in appearance over time. From tumbled textures with old-world appeal to slick, polished surfaces, stone can blend in quietly or make a bold design statement.

As you read this section, consider the possibilities stone offers as an alternative to brick, concrete, and wood. Get inspired! After all, the backyard is a vacationland in many ways—an outdoor living room that lures us away from the daily hubbub and into a relaxing place.

To begin the design process, unearth ideas from these pages and any other sources you may have and then incorporate them into your own landscape plan. Then, turn your attention to the techniques section of the book and prepare to begin the transformation from everyday backyard into a great escape.

RIVER ROCK IN VARIOUS SIZES and shapes serves as a loose, hardscape groundcover surrounding a pond. The combination of stone size, shape, color, and texture adds interest that a homogenous surface cannot accomplish.

Design Concepts

Because most stonescape installations aren't perennial features that you can easily uproot, thoughtful planning should precede any stone project. Hardscape is generally the first order of business with landscape design. Once you figure out the framework, then you can add color and texture with plants. The process for planning your outdoor space is no different than building a home. First you lay the foundation, and later you can install extras like window treatments and throw rugs. Think of your landscape as a book with multiple chapters. Take projects one at a time.

Start by looking through the projects in this book, and refer to magazines for ideas. You won't fall short of inspiration with the variety of gardening publications available today. All of them show stone used in many applications. Take a trip to the stoneyard and see what materials are available. How might the color,

texture, and character of various selections fit into your landscape? This preliminary visit to check out materials options can spark stonescaping ideas for your backyard.

If you have never laid a patio or worked with stone in any capacity, consider starting small. Choose a project that has some "give" and requires little cutting and shaping of stone—and a design that requires less arithmetic. A stepping stone pathway is a great starter project that has extensive creative possibilities in stone type and placement, utilization of groundcover, gravel, and other landscaping to frame the stones. There's always room to advance to patio projects that involve manufactured cobblestones or flagstones; continue incorporating stone into the landscape by using it to build a fire pit or to border a pond. Techniques in this book will guide you through the steps as you design and build with stone.

STONE IS A PRACTICAL, safe groundcover for a fire pit area, as well as the only practical material for making the pit itself.

Function

Before you put pen to paper, spend time seriously considering how you will use your space. What outdoor activities do you enjoy? One homeowner's backyard might serve as an informal sports arena, while another uses the space as a quiet refuge. Each will choose different patio arrangements. Someone with a large family who hosts barbecue gatherings will go to the drawing table with different expectations than a townhouse dweller who just acquired a first, compact plot of land. It's noteworthy to mention: Stone is great in small spaces.

Will you need lots of outdoor "flooring" for patio furniture and a kitchen area, or will a small patio space that serves as a walk-out to your garden suffice? What other landscape elements require stone treatment? Ponds, fire pits, retaining walls, and walkways are a few examples. If you have the luxury of starting from scratch with your design, you can make allowances for these features as you plan, creating several phases to your design so you can space out your projects over several year's time.

Most of us are not working with a clean canvas. We are either improving a backyard that doesn't function as we wish, upgrading a deck to a stone patio, or adding

A STONE VENEER FINISH on this townhouse complex complements wood siding. Homeowners considering a patio might carry out this theme with a tumbled concrete paver surface.

a retaining wall here, and a walkway there to enhance the existing space. Consider the materials used in your backyard, the color scheme, and the style of your plantings. Do you prefer formal, trimmed shrubbery or a wild, cottage garden? These style clues will help you determine what type of stone is most appropriate for your landscape.

THIS WINDING STONE MORTAR WALL is an important architectural element on the property, accenting the home's entryway façade.

Style

A traditional, center-hall colonial house with manicured gardens calls for an entirely different approach to stonescape than a rustic, log-cabin home or a modern townhouse with a courtyard. Architectural style is an important factor in stone selection. A tidy, concrete-paver brick entrance is more appropriate for the conservative home, while a patch-worked fieldstone path suits a natural setting.

However, the way stone materials are treated in a landscape can make all the difference. Fine gravel paths are formal when contained in a tidy walkway. In a Zen garden, this same pea-sized stone surface lends a modern appeal. Remember, the material you choose, whether natural or manufactured, should work in harmony with the setting and style of your home.

Topography

As you determine where to place a patio, locate a wall, or lay a path, do not ignore your own private microclimate. Your yard has sunny spots and shady areas. It has some places where soil is soggy and others where dirt is so dry that nothing will grow. Managing soil is a significant

A JAPANESE-INSPIRED LANDSCAPE benefits from this collection of uniquely shaped boulders.

Take inventory of your table, chairs, grill, and other patio furniture. Most people underestimate the square footage required to comfortably fit all of these items into one space. You don't want to be bumping elbows. You may require a multi-level patio, or a second "secret garden" patio for relaxing.

element in the success of patio, wall, or path design. It is, after all, the foundation that will brace tons of weight, or at least several hundred pounds. Examine your property—really take a look. You will need to address foundation issues with each project.

Slope is another topographical characteristic that will rule the way you build steps, a patio, and retaining walls. Your land may slope away from your home down to a lower area, perhaps a creek bed. Or the land may slope just slightly toward your home. You will recognize

this condition after a hard rain if water collects by your home's foundation. (Not a good situation if you want to avoid a wet basement, cracking walls, or settling that can damage the structure.) You need to measure the slope of your yard to determine if you need to do any grading work before you begin prepping the foundation or laying stone. You may hire a surveyor to accurately assess the grade of your property; and you can also refer to your property plat, which is generally available at your city hall or through a municipal building department.

THIS PROPERTY WILL REQUIRE GRADING to create a proper foundation for a patio. A multi-level patio with various "rooms" for cooking, dining, and relaxing would suit the sloped property.

COLOR IS A CONTROLLABLE PART of your stonescape planning. Both natural and manmade stone materials come in very vibrant colors that make a strong statement, or in muted tones that offer a more relaxed feeling.

Color

Pavers and gravel come in a rainbow of colors, making the landscape supply house a candy store for anyone who wants to make a statement in his or her yard. You'll find blends and finishes that mimic natural stone in color and texture—resembling sandstone or bluestone, for instance. Actually, you can buy pavers made from natural sandstone or bluestone (see page 42). The key to color is to consider what would naturally appear in your landscape—what stones are native to your region? These pavers will look the most at home in your landscape. If sandstone is common in your area, you may lean toward concrete pavers that display more yellow tones. In areas where manmade stonescape such as red brick is prevalent, continue the tradition with red-hued pavers that recall the existing brickwork.

If you want the stonescape to blend with your environment, your best bet is to lean toward natural, neutral colors. For instance, steer clear of stark-white gravel or lava-red rocks for a walkway to your home if your goal is to blend. Keep it subtle. The idea is to guide people from point A to point B, highlighting your home or a garden in the distance, not the path one must walk to arrive there. If the stonescape is not the focal point, tone it down. Also remember when choosing color, the single paver you see as a sample will make a greater impact when it appears *en masse*.

Precast concrete pavers

Pavers finished with colorful exposed aggregate are another option for adding new tones and textures into your landscape. Made of cast concrete and sold in both square and round shapes, these pavers are very inexpensive.

Typically between 1 and 1½" (25 to 38 mm) in thickness, they are somewhat prone to breakage and their relatively porous nature makes them susceptible to water and freeze/thaw damage.

Texture

The value of stone is second to none when it comes to its ability to turn a boring surface into a rich canvas of texture and color. Stone's texture adds variety to a landscape, and it lends definition to a flat surface. Natural stone has nuances like ripples and dimples. Manufactured pavers can look tumbled and "Old World," or grainy and slick. They can be cut neatly into perfect slabs or artificially aged. Depending on the finish you choose, stone can look rugged or as tidy and formal as an indoor space. You can find natural bluestone that is uniformly colored and as polished looking as the tile you would lay in a grand foyer. Laying a checkerboard pattern of limestone or sandstone gives an outdoor kitchen the appearance that a "floor" was put in place. Because stone and pavers introduce dimension to the landscape, they blend with other elements outdoors. Mother Nature just isn't perfect, so incorporating stone with worn and earthen textures complements the beauty of outdoors rather than forcing in an element that seems too "fake."

Speaking of which, concrete and clay pavers available today don't fall short in the texture department. New can look old. You'll find manufactured pavers by names like Rivenstone, which resembles bluestone flags with its pitched edges, and Courtstone, with a rounded shape that mimics weathered, basalt cobblestones found in Europe. You can also go for colored pavers with a smooth finish and create a surface pattern. Don't tie yourself to one texture. You can lay a border in one paver type, and fill a patio with another. As you choose a stone texture, consider the location of the surface. You may decide to avoid jagged, rough surfaces in high-traffic areas where pedestrians may trip (walkways).

THE NOOKS AND CRANNIES inherent in cut natural stone provide textural interest to a garden. Here, the hard lines of this retaining wall are softened by the colorful impact of a rose bowing over its surface.

A BRICK BORDER neatly outlines this natural bluestone walkway, laid in a variation of the running bond pattern (see page 45).

Paths & Walkways

The purpose of paths and walkways in the landscape is twofold: to visually connect various "rooms" and features; and to map out sensible, accessible and comfortable walk routes from point A to point B—that is, from patio to garden, from sidewalk to front porch. A utilitarian approach is to lay a path for safety reasons, creating a clear-cut pedestrian runway that is meant to purposefully usher people to a destination. But many paths are much more than a means to an end. Your path will communicate to visitors where to go and how to get there. A less formal path will encourage a slower pace, forcing exploration. Stepping stones artfully placed in a garden will merely suggest a trail through a crowd of plant-life. You'll eventually find the treasure at the end of the trail—prize roses, a gurgling fountain. The pleasure is in the journey.

While designing a path and considering materials for these projects, consider the experience you want people to have as they navigate the walkway. Do you want to guide them quickly without distraction, or do you hope they'll discover a cozy sitting area along the way? With your goals in mind, you can begin to sketch a roadmap.

COLOR OUTSIDE THE LINES. A straight line is a safe and efficient form for a pathway, but adding a few jogs and bends adds great visual interest.

A STEPPING STONE WALKWAY allows grass "grout" to grow. A path is important for guiding the eye, and foot traffic, through a landscape.

A PEBBLE PATHWAY contained by a loose-laid brick border provides just enough tracking for people to safely meander through a woodland backyard.

Think of a path as a mini highway system for your yard. You may only require a single walkway that leads from a side garage door, around the house, to the deck out back. Or, your landscape design may include pockets of interest that you want people to discover: a pond, gazebo, bench, garden, or children's play area. In this case, you'll need some "side streets" or back roads. Your main artery will probably serve as a safe route with the sheer purpose of clearing the way for pedestrians. Pathways may branch off of this key walkway. These are the scenic byways.

Materials

Choose materials and structure your paths according to their purpose and your design preferences. Brick, flagstone, concrete pavers, and gravel are popular choices for paths. Their surfaces aren't completely smooth, promoting skid resistance that allows for safe traction. If you opt for stepping stones, be sure you consider the natural stride of everyone who will use the path regularly. Placing them just an inch too far apart can trip up walkers. (You can walk across concrete with wet feet and measure your stride to determine functional stepping stone placement.) On the other hand, if you simply want to establish a less defined walking zone, you can play with the arrangement of stepping stones and create interesting designs.

Brick, flagstone, gravel, and concrete pavers are readily available and can be formal or casual depending on how you design the path. For instance, mortared flagstone tends to look somewhat formal, while flagstone set on sand does not. Lay flagstone on a prepared, earthen surface and you can plant rock-loving groundcover varieties such as creeping thyme and moss in between the cracks. Manufactured brick will offer a uniform, clean look. Natural brick has color variances. Recycled brick will blend well in mature landscapes and also provide a rustic look. Decorative stepping stones can jazz up a gravel path.

Before committing to a material for your walkway surface, ask yourself these questions:

- How regularly will you use this path?
- What other materials exist in your landscape? (Think patio, retaining walls, etc.)
- What materials will complement your home's architecture?
- Describe the setting: formal, casual, rustic-country, private, highly visible, etc.
- Who will walk on this path, and do they have special needs? (An even flagstone pathway is safer to traverse than a less uniform walkway of aggregate stone.)
- What are the site conditions? Is the area particularly soggy and prone to puddling? (Stone gets slippery when wet. And wet stone is a welcome environment for moss, which compounds the slick factor.)

Test Your Ideas

Before setting a project in stone, quite literally, test your projects by cutting models from scrap cardboard or even paper. For instance, when creating a stepping stone path, test layouts with cardboard templates before purchasing real stone. It is easy to miscalculate the quantity of materials required to complete a project. Same goes with size. You may be surprised how large a stepping stone must be to look substantial on your property. Meanwhile, as you use your cardboard steppers to lay out the path, test placement and be sure to arrange the stones to conform to your stride.

SUITABLE MATERIALS FOR PATHWAYS include interlocking pavers, cobblestones, flagstones, and gravel. For gravel pathways, choose small aggregates ⅜ to ¾" (1- to 1.9 cm). The texture looks appealing, and if you choose a variety of sizes and shapes the surface will stay in place. Interlocking pavers have shapes and protrusions that are designed to fit together and create a mechanical bond. Square and rectangular pavers and cobblestones are easier to lay out in a pathway. Flagstones can be laid in a solid pattern or used as stepping stones.

A TAMPED FIRM BASE with good drainage is vital to a successful pathway project. Compactible gravel makes an excellent base.

PATHWAYS NORMALLY REQUIRE A BORDER to contain the surfacing material and create a mowing edge. Brick pavers can be laid flat or buried deeper on end (called soldier style).

Base & Borders

We'll delve into the specifics of preparing the base for your path in later sections of this book, but for now let's underscore the importance of setting a solid foundation. Whether your path is purely for foot traffic or primarily a decorative statement (most often, the goal is both of these), you must take steps to secure the base and plan for drainage. You won't need to install culverts or hire the Army Corps of Engineers for this task. A simple half-inch (1.3 cm) slope from the center of your path to its edges will direct water away from the middle, preventing puddles and unsafe, slippery conditions. This is called crowning. You'll notice that your street is slightly crowned, directing water toward the curb and into drainage grates. You will need a similar, much smaller-scale, system for you landscape path.

Next, consider how you will edge your path. A decorative border is optional, but it allows another opportunity to mix and match materials so as to marry the many different materials used throughout the landscape. For example, if your patio is composed of tumbled concrete pavers, but your home has stone accents, you can create a stone path with a brick border to bring the contrasting surfaces together. Play with the possibilities. Install a brick border along a gravel path, place native rock boulders alongside a sandstone path, or set stone slabs alongside a path of cobbled concrete pavers. Play with different textures and colors as well.

Aside from brick and stone, consider other ways to define your path. Hedges establish an attractive green border, while plastic edging available at home centers will do a fine job of preventing plants and turf from invading your walkway.

Before you begin any structural project, consult your local building department for information on building permits, codes, and other applicable laws.

Walls & Steps

Walls and steps perform multiple functions of blocking views, dividing spaces, connecting different levels, and improving access. They are functional focal points. A system of walls along a slope, called retaining walls, carves out tiered plant beds. Even a short wall of brick or stone will provide privacy and set clear boundaries between your lot and the neighbor's, or between a private patio and the rest of your yard.

In sloped areas, a stone staircase is a logical alternative to a path, which may be too steep to walk safely.

Especially if you plan to use gravel, you'll want to eliminate the effects of gravity from the design. Plain gravel won't stay put on a steep slope, and you'll wind up skidding down the surface. For this reason, steps are often a safety-first solution. Plus, landing stairs are convenient niches to display container plantings, and you may incorporate a few large landings that step down from one patio level to the next. In this way, steps are another feature for creating separate living spaces in the landscape.

PAVERS ARE MADE FROM NATURAL STONE or are cast. Their uniform shape and size ease the installation process.

Designing Walls

Walls can accompany stairs, enclose a patio, or frame a garden—but they also can stand alone. Walls are a powerful design tool for creating physical and mental barriers. They can conceal unappealing yard features from the rest of the garden. They set limits, draw lines, divide property. They are an ample platform for growing vines, and if they're short enough, walls are handy overflow seating if you're hosting a large patio party.

When deciding on a wall style and material, consider the visual impact of this feature. Walls make a statement, and their appearance will set the tone in your landscape. A tidy brick-paver wall sends a different message than a dry stacked fieldstone structure. A wall composed of natural stone blends with the landscape.

The paths and steps you build should complement walls. Regarding materials, you can go natural with dry stacked fieldstone, ashlar (typical, blocky wall stone), or choose among an array of manufactured "interlocking" products. (See Planting Your Retaining Wall on page 147.)

A DRY-STACKED FIELDSTONE WALL in the country looks as though it grew right out of the earth. Natural stone belongs in the environment, and it harmonizes with other landscape elements, such as the stone walkway seen here.

Dry Stacked Walls

Walls may be built using mortar to bind the stones, or they may be dry-stacked. Your climate, wall dimensions, and materials will dictate the best construction method. Mortared walls usually require a reinforced concrete footing poured below the frost line so the wall does not flex and crack at the joints. To further prevent freeze/thaw damage, keep water out of a mortar wall by topping the structure with capstones, which helps seal the top of the wall and thus limit water penetration. Mortar allows you to meld together interesting and rounded, decorative stones that need sticking power. Sealing seams between rock layers will not allow plants to peek through, which can be a pro or con, depending on your desire for the overall effect.

Not all walls require mortar, and you may prefer the aged-and-tumbled look of a dry stacked wall. These walls do not require a poured concrete base since they can flex with the movement of the earth without cracking. Dry stacked walls freely accommodate freeze-and-thaw cycles. Constructing such a wall is like piecing together a complex puzzle: no two pieces are truly a fit until you cut and rearrange stones, wedge slivers into gaps, and artfully create a continuous surface. If you're not up for the challenge, you can hire a professional.

TUMBLED CONCRETE WALL BLOCK can blend almost seamlessly with a patio or walkway made of similar material.

SHORT WALLS WITH ONLY A FEW LAYERS OF STONE may not require mortar. Because these cast stones are flat and uniform in size, they offer sturdy construction in a dry-stacked structure.

MANUFACTURED INTERLOCKING BLOCKS have revolutionized the manner in which retaining walls are built. Once limited to buff colors and a rough, split texture, interlocking blocks are being made in a rapidly increasing array of styles, sizes, and colors.

Retaining Walls

As the name suggests, a retaining wall holds back soil. In essence, a retaining wall turns a slope into a plateau-and-drop. Rather than a steep grade, you have a flat-planed surface supported by a sturdy wall. This allows you to readily use the flat space for planting, placing furniture, or even laying a patio. The dramatic drop adds interest and utility to a landscape. A common technique for long, sloped yards is to install several stepped-down retaining walls, creating earthen landings that break up the slope into manageable sections.

When building a stone retaining wall, you can use natural materials or interlocking blocks designed for the express purpose of stacking. Either can bear the weight of the heavy soil being retained, but cast blocks are DIY-friendly, durable, and easier on your wallet than natural stone. You can purchase interlocking blocks with natural finishes that blend better with the environment. You don't need to worry about shaping stone because the flat tops and bottoms of interlocking blocks are smooth and ready to stack.

You can go natural with materials and opt for ashlar that has been split into rectangular blocks. Stacked fieldstone accomplishes a rustic look. A row of boulders is an artistic way to create a boundary.

INTERLOCKING BLOCKS COME READY TO STACK. You can purchase tumbled and treated blocks with natural faces that blend into your backyard environment. Some blocks, like these, resemble stacked limestone.

A SLOPED PROPERTY is addressed by building a system of concrete walls faced with stone veneer to create multiple levels and places to plant.

Designing Steps

A spiral staircase is the centerpiece of a grand home's foyer, capturing interest with its sturdy but elegant architecture. Steps in a landscape perform the same magic.

Steps are often placed in conjunction with retaining walls and paths. In sequence, it's best to build steps and retaining walls together, and then paths. That way, you can align a path's grade to that of the landing step. You don't want to deconstruct portions of your wall to accommodate a staircase.

Push boundaries when choosing materials for steps. You can start with the basic timber and gravel project on page 91. But other options include using large stone slabs as steps set into the earth. A cobbled stone or paver veneer laid over concrete steps is both sturdy and rich with character. Flat, streamlined flagstones are a popular choice and, again, you can opt for manufactured products that interlock neatly.

A word on design: a stairway doesn't need to be straight. Steps positioned in a zig-zag as they escalate break up a vertical monotony and when set up as switchbacks can decrease slope. A curved stairway gives a patio and boxy backyard more depth and motion. Consider stacked, circle-shaped steps, neat brick stairs, and large stepping stones positioned on the incline. Each requires proper footing, and knowledge of rise and run.

A LANDING breaks up a stairway and creates a small gathering space.

YOU CAN SEEK OUT NATURAL STONE from creek beds or construction sites where the earth has been turned over and rock exposed. A supplier has access to myriad stone varieties and sizes. Seek out rock types that are typically found in your region for the most natural look.

STONE FLAGS SET LIKE TILE offer smoother texture and a more formal appearance.

BOULDERS PERFORM A VITAL DESIGN FUNCTION in Zen spaces like this one.

Accents & Accessories

The versatility of stone in its many forms—ashlar, boulder, slab, gravel, and others—allows it to blend with the surroundings. It can subtly work its job as a path, wall, steps, or any other functional landscape element without drawing unnecessary attention. Stone is just as natural. Though just as stone easily slips into an environmental backdrop, it can stand out as the main event in a landscape design. A trio of granite river rock boulders stationed in a contemporary, Japanese-inspired "green garden" of foliage plants is a dynamic focal point. There are numerous examples of using stone in ways that both camouflage and call out its character. Following are some ideas to get you started. Once you begin to explore stoneyards and work with the material in various capacities, you'll begin to discover new ways to use stone as an accessory and an accent.

Stone as Furniture

Stone is a sturdy, timeless building material with a track record that goes back to prehistoric days. We continue the tradition of using stone, one pallet at a time, as a component for constructing outdoor features. But a single stone slab is highly functional as a solo act. A concrete paver will serve as a functional side-table top, paired with a base made from a ceramic flower pot or even a tree trunk. On a larger scale, a dining table-sized sandstone slab is a rustic alternative to basic patio furniture.

As you discover various stone cuts and boulder options at your local stoneyard, you will run across a piece that would be a perfect garden stool, or a slab that would work as a bench. Some naturally harvested stones contain bumps and grooves that are in just the right places. Aside from stone tabletops and benches, a modest-sized boulder provides an interesting place to engrave your house address. Place it in a plant bed by your door. A boulder with a deep center groove can be converted into a planter with very rustic appeal.

A ROCK CHAIR formed with flagstone and ashlar is a charming, functional focal point in the garden.

Stone as Landscape

Rock is the ultimate low-maintenance landscape material. If your idea of the perfect landscape is to set it and forget it, then you can't beat stone and stone products, including concrete brick pavers and an eclectic family of manufactured slabs. You can virtually eliminate mowing by arranging decorative sandstone pavers in a grid-like pattern. Think of rows of stones with moss or creeping thyme serving as living mortar.

Gravel and pebble products also can serve as the foundation for an entire garden. You can choose smooth river rock to border a pond area and fill a space next to a patio, or opt for different sizes of decorative rock for beds. Succulents can survive in this environment. Gravel is screened and separated so you can purchase a load of uniformly sized pieces. In the case of a Zen garden, a base of pea gravel or pebble stone forms a surface that is raked smooth. A single boulder or a grouping may sit on this base to serve as natural artwork.

PAVERS MAKE A STRONG IMPACT in large surface areas, especially when laid in circular and curved patterns. They don't require water, fertilizer, or care, other than a good sweeping to brush off leaves in the fall.

Rock Gardens

Rock gardens can be positioned on sloped lawns, in shady areas, or in places where grass simply refuses to grow. Choose a cohesive group of different rock shapes, sizes, and textures. Think of your rock garden as a puzzle. Alternate shapes and sizes to add interest. Notice how rocks interlock, how their grooves support and hold one another in place when arranged with a careful eye.

While you can visit a quarry and hand-pick stones, you may also find free rocks in your own backyard. When choosing rocks for your garden, keep in mind their porosity. You can tell by their mass: Are they dense and heavy? The reason you'll want to include some porous rocks in your garden is because they weather more quickly, forming a mossy patina that gives the impression that they are veterans in your landscape, not stark brand-new additions. Foliage plants that peek between rocks in your garden will offer year-round color. Choose low-growing, clumping varieties like hens and chicks (sepervivum tectorum) and taller, leafy plants like

Rock Garden Picks

Top rock: A sandstone that is generally wider than it is tall; stacks well; has a natural, weathered appearance; tan in color.

Red sandstone: Porous; attractive red color; crumbly, weathered-looking rock.

Moss rock: Dense, thin sandstone; dark in color; ideal for retaining walls.

Weathered limestone: Sedimentary rock; available in small and large pieces; also available as boulders.

Lava rock: Commonly found in Zen gardens; porous rock; lightweight; contrasts nicely with white gravel; artistic shapes serve as accent pieces; purchased individually from quarries; sold by the pound (so purchase these rocks when dry so you aren't paying for water that can double the weight of the stones).

lamb's ears (stachys byzantina). You can tuck in annuals that are appropriate for your climate zone.

A WEATHERED LIMESTONE ROCK FORMATION makes a striking statement in this densely wooded yard.

Specimen Stones

Large, distinctive stones can serve as simple stone landscape features, like statuary or bird baths, as well as performing roles as fire pits, the pillars of an arbor garden entrance, an earthen rim on ponds, and the body of a bubbling fountain.

Despite significant mass, boulders will move with the earth. They will shift with freeze-and-thaw cycles if set above the frost line. For a completely stationary boulder arrangement—think a trio of different shaped boulders in a Japanese garden—you'll need to dig below your local frost level. (The ground will freeze to a different depth depending on where you live.) Otherwise, bury at least one-third of a tall boulder or ledge stone for stability. Even squat boulders should be buried below the point at which they slope back toward the center. This way, they look like a part of the landscape. Also, choose native rock so the boulders don't look as if they dropped from outer space.

ROCK FORMED INTO A WATER FEATURE will eventually weather from the constant moisture, adding character to the man-made waterfall.

LAVA ROCK SPECIMEN STONES dot this quiet Japanese sanctuary, breaking up an open field.

Stonescaping Materials

A stoneyard is a candy store for inspired do-it-yourselfers who have a plan in hand. The stone products available today, both natural and manufactured, allow us to lay flooring and build walls that are every bit as appealing as what we find indoors. Whether you choose to work with natural stone—sourcing regional varieties that look as though they've been a part of your landscape for decades—or you opt for pavers that are convenient to install, you will discover textures, colors, and shapes that complement your space. Here's all you need to know about stone, and what tools will help you get the job done.

Natural Stone

Every stone tells a geological story of what lies beneath; every specimen is a regional expression. Granite fieldstone harvested in New England is found in the characteristic country walls you'll find along the seaboard. This material would be a peculiar transplant in your Midwestern backyard if you live in an area where native sandstone and limestone make a more natural statement. Though just about any type of rock can be ordered and shipped, you should always ask yourself the question: Does this rock really belong here?

A visit to a local stoneyard will reveal the various cuts and types of natural stone available, the many shapes and sizes, and all the color variations. As you explore the options for the stonescape projects in this book, you'll work with various types and forms of rock. This primer will help you select appropriate stone materials and ask informed questions while shopping at a stoneyard.

Despite the selection of manufactured paver products on the market today, there are many reasons you may prefer to work with natural stone. First, there's the authenticity of real stone—texture and colors that will never be perfectly reproduced in a manmade product. While there are some close ringers, when arranged side by side, natural stone and a manufactured counterpart are easily distinguished. Stone is just as much part of our outdoor environment as native plants, age-old trees, and the soil we walk on. Even when we intentionally arrange stone in our landscapes, using it as building material for creature comforts like fire pits or patios, it still blends completely as a natural part of the environment. Meanwhile, by embracing the imperfections in natural stone—odd shapes, rough edges—we can add character to landscape features.

TUCKED INTO THE CREVICES of this fieldstone sitting area are rock-loving plants like moss and creeping thyme that add color and interest to the space.

Rock Basics

You can categorize rock two ways: by stone type and form. The dominant three types of rock are igneous, sedimentary, and metamorphic rock.

Igneous rock is solidified magma. Magma is composed of minerals in molten form, from hot fire deep in the earth's core. As magma pushes closer to ground level, it hardens to form igneous rock, the oldest kind. Igneous rock cools in different ways. Intrusive igneous rock, such as granite, contains large crystals and cools slowly below ground level. Extrusive igneous rock forms when volcano lava dries and hardens. When extrusive rock cools quickly, it creates a shiny black rock without crystals, such as obsidian. When it cools more slowly, allowing small crystals to develop, a fine-grained rock such as basalt is formed.

Sedimentary rock consists of layer upon layer of mud, sand, gravel, clay, quartz, and microorganisms. When these particles are swept up by wind and rain, they collect at the surface in places like beaches and river-beds. Over time, these sediments compact and another layer, or strata, forms on top. Sedimentary rock is divided into three types based on its contents: clastic, organic, and chemical. Clastic rocks are primarily formed from broken bits and pieces off other rock. Examples include sandstone, shale, and quartz. Organic sedimentary rock, such as limestone, forms from remains of living things like plankton and plants. Chemical sedimentary rock consists of hardened layers of mineral crystals that are formed when seas dry up and salty contents are left behind. The result is halite, gypsum, and sea salt.

Metamorphic rock was once igneous or sedimentary, but the pressure and heat buildup beneath the earth's surface changes them. The pressure is from thick layers of rock—miles of it—squeezing down upon itself: Limestone morphs into marble, shale turns into slate, and sandstone becomes quartzite.

Natural Stonescaping

Limestone

Granite

Sandstone

Slate

Limestone: Heavy stone, moderately easy to cut, medium to high strength, used in garden walls, rock gardens, walks, steps, and patios. Major U.S. sources: Indiana, Wisconsin, Kansas, and Texas.

Granite: Dense, heavy stone, difficult to cut, used for paving walks and building steps and walls; the most widely used building stone. Major U.S. sources: Massachusetts, Georgia, Minnesota, North Carolina, South Dakota, and Vermont.

Sandstone: Relatively lightweight stone available in "soft" and "dense" varieties and a wide range of colors. Soft sandstone is easier to cut, but also lower in strength; used in garden walls, especially in frost-free climates. Major U.S. sources: New York, Arizona, Ohio, and Pennsylvania.

Slate: Fine, medium-weight stone that is soft and easy to cut, but low in strength; too brittle for wall construction, but a popular choice for walks, steps and patios; colors vary widely from region to region. Major U.S. sources: Pennsylvania, Virginia, Vermont, Maine, New York, and Georgia.

Stone Forms

Stone form refers to the shape and cut of the rock. Form is critical as you take on projects in this book. Ashlar (1) is blocky, cut wall stone that is either rough or finely shaped into stackable pieces. You can find ashlar in various heights and widths. Flagstone (2) is essentially large, flat rock that can be installed as a patio or walkway or used as steppers. You may hear flagstone casually referred to as "flags." These rocks are split on the grain and generally measure two to three inches thick and are usually quite large. If you want flagstones that are less unwieldy, you should ask for stepping stones, the smaller cousin. These are ideal for pathways. For patios, ask for flagstone or steppers.

Fieldstones (3) originate in regions with rocky soil. As opposed to quarrying the stone, fieldstones are harvested from the natural environment. They are plucked out of one setting, and sold as fieldstone for your use. These stones are like mini boulders, rounded and smooth from weathering; you'll find them in irregular shapes and various sizes. Do not confuse fieldstone with rubble, which are also irregular but of lesser quality. Rubble (4) has its place in the landscape: as filler in dry stacked walls, for instance. However, you probably wouldn't use rubble as the feature material in a project. Fieldstone and its cousin river rock may be sold crushed for use as a drainage layer or top-dressing.

1. Ashlar

2. Flagstone

Patios: Flagstone or stepping stones (smaller slabs); common varieties are sandstone and bluestone.

Walls/Retaining walls: Ashlar (wall stone) in a native stone, such as limestone; fieldstone and rubble (for filler); boulders.

Paths: Flagstone; stepping stones.

Decorative: Boulders; specimen stone like ledgestone; slabs of native stone, such as granite.

3. Crushed Fieldstone

While exploring the stoneyard, you'll also come across specimen stones, which vary by region. A ledgestone blasted out from a river bluff can be imported into your Zen garden as a natural centerpiece. Some boulders are also specimen stones, harvested for their unique shapes, textures, and other character traits. You can actually build walls from boulders, using rubble as a form of loose mortar to fill large gaps. Shims or wedge-shaped stones are also used for this purpose. Veener stone (5) is used in cosmetic applications, such as facing exterior walls or freestanding concrete block walls.

4. Rubble

5. Veneer Stone

QUICK TIP: STONEYARD CALCULATIONS

As you browse through the stoneyard, you'll find stacks of stone baskets brimming with interesting specimens—no two are alike. It's tempting to remove stones from their storage places to take a closer look at the texture, color, or unique markings. Ask a sales associate to help first. Oftentimes, the baskets and pallets you see are pre-weighed to sell. Taking a single rock from the pile can throw off the stoneyard's calculations.

STONE AND BRICK SUPPLIERS typically have a showroom with samples that are easy to browse and knowledgeable sales staff on the floor.

A Visit to the Stoneyard

A trip to a local stoneyard can be an inspiring start to any stonescaping project. You'll find pallets of quarried flagstone, cut stone that's perfect for a formal patio, piles of fieldstone and rubble for dry stacked walls, and a satisfying array of rock forms and sizes. Many stoneyards also sell concrete pavers and bricks. While you're checking out the inventory, take notes, snap pictures if you must, and ask lots of questions of professionals. They can guide you toward appropriate materials for your projects.

First, a word on buying local. When you source stone from outside your region, you can slap on extra costs for shipping and delivery. Native rock is more readily available, so it's affordable, plentiful—you won't run out

How Much Do You Need?

Before you visit a stoneyard, determine how much area you plan to cover—literally. Know the dimensions of your project: height, width, length. Convert this into square footage. For a wall, you will multiply the length and height to arrive at a measurement. This number will help a professional calculate how much stone you should buy, always allowing for extra.

and wind up with a patchwork landscape—and it blends with your environment. In most every case, buying local stone is the way to go.

What to Look For

Now you're ready to select stone for projects. Be sure to evaluate color, texture, uniformity, and durability. Additionally, consider the following qualities for the following stone forms:

ASHLAR: This blocky wall stone should be consistent in thickness with neatly trimmed edges and flat sides so stone will stack easily. Ashlar comes in various sizes, and you'll need to choose a range of larger stones for the foundation, long stones to form the body of the wall, and some flat cap stones for the top.

BOULDERS: Depending on how you plan to use boulders in the landscape, you may seek out uniformly shaped rocks for a high-impact wall, or a group of interesting boulders in different heights and shapes for a garden centerpiece. If the latter is your goal, go ahead and mix shapes and sizes but be sure to choose boulders of the same specimen. Consistency in rock type is key. Be on the lookout for interesting colors, textures, and highlights. At the stoneyard, ask for a hose or a waterbucket so you can wash the boulders and see their true colors.

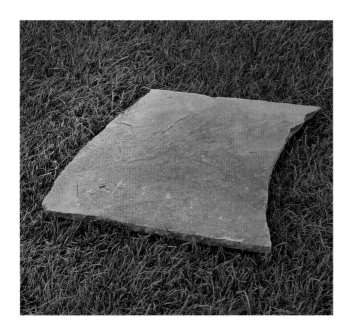

FLAGSTONE: Look for consistency in thickness. Otherwise, you will compensate later by having to adjust how you set the stone into your subbase. You'll find flagstone in various textures, some more flat and others ridged. In some applications, an interesting surface is more important than a smooth texture. In others, such as a walkway that will get heavy foot traffic, you may decide that an even texture is a priority. Inspect the rock, overall, and determine its durability. Also evaluate the color to see whether it will complement your home, existing landscape features, and your property's surroundings. You'll evaluate similar qualities in stepping stones and cut stone.

LOOSE MATERIALS USED IN STONESCAPING INCLUDE: **(A)** Smooth river rock for top dressing; **(B)** crushed rock for stable surface dressing; **(C)** crushed quartz for decorative top dressing; **(D)** trap rock for well-drained subbases or decorative top dressing (not a good choice for walking surfaces); **(E)** crushed limestone for subbases and top dressing; **(F)** small-diameter river rock for top dressing and drainage; **(G)** pea gravel for top dressing; **(H)** compactable gravel (class V or class II) for compacted subbases; **(I)** coarse sand for paver beds; **(J)** fine sand for gap-filling; **(K)** black dirt for backfilling.

Gravel, Sand & Dirt

Gravel, sand, and black dirt are essential building materials for any landscaping project. In smaller quantities, you can obtain these materials in poly bags at garden or building centers. For larger amounts, pay a visit to a landscape supply outlet and purchase them by the cubic yard or by the ton.

Gravel is essentially a chip off the rock—mechanically broken-down stone that has numerous applications in the landscape. You may spread it as surface material, such as in the gravel-and-timber stairs project (see page 90). Gravel is a convenient material for paths, and you can use it as "carpet" in a Zen garden, or as a buffer in drainage zones, such as against the home.

When choosing gravel, consider the project and setting. Follow the rules of proportion. Large, angled gravel is appropriate against a house and will stand up to broad building details. Pea-sized gravel fits in a Zen or rock garden, not detracting from larger stone focal points. Also, match gravel to other stones in the garden and other

features in the environment. Choose a buff limestone with hints of yellow for a path by your yellow home.

Gravel ranges in diameter from 2 inches (5.1 cm) to ¼-inch (6 mm). Gravel is characterized as crushed or smooth. Gravel size is regulated through a screening process. For instance, ¾-inch (1.9-cm) river rock sifted through a screen with ¾-inch (1.9-cm) holes will prevent larger material from passing through. A second screen with a finer grid will allow grainier bits to pass, preserving the consistent, ¾-inch gravel size.

Black dirt sold at landscape centers usually is pulverized and sterilized. This is fine for backfilling, but if you are planting you'll want to amend the soil. Dirt is normally sold by the cubic yard since the weight varies dramatically based on the moisture content.

Sand generally is sold in two types: coarse building sand and fine sand for landscaping or sandboxes. Extremely fine sand, such as blasting medium for sandblasting, has no use in stonescaping or landscaping.

Angular gravels are sold by type and size. For instance, ¾" (1.9-cm) St. Cloud Granite is a type of granite rock that was crushed and screened to a ¾" diameter. You'll find consistency in the color and size of this gravel.

If gravel is river rock, its surface will be smooth, rounded, shiny, and variegated in color. This material is more likely to roll around and shift on the surface than an angled gravel with jagged edges that produces friction and stays put. Also, angular gravel is made by crushing one type of rock, so the color is consistent.

Most likely, you will have gravel delivered by the supplier. An important tip to remember: Ask that it is spread on a hard, flat surface like your driveway. The best way to scoop gravel is by sliding a flat shovel under the edge of the pile. This is difficult to accomplish if the gravel pile is in a corner of your backyard. Often, however, sand and gravel are delivered in large parachute style bags that limit migration but can make it difficult to shovel up the dregs of the pile.

Now, take the screening process we described earlier, and eliminate the second part—the removal of "fines" that are smaller than the screen size. Fines are crushed

Estimating Gravel

Calculate how much gravel you need by measuring the area. (You may wait until after placing edging to get accurate area measurements.) Divide your area into "boxes," or sections. Measure the volume of each, and figure out the sum of these boxes. Convert inches to cubic feet. For instance: 2" x 10' x 6' = 10 cf. Your supplier can make adjustments if they sell by the yard or by the ton.

particles that can be grains or silt. This material is sifted out of single-size gravels (like that ¾-inch river rock). You'll see this material referred to as paver base, class V, road base, hard core, ¾-minus, or other regional variations. Compactable gravel is used to create a stable subbase.

Hauling Materials

You can save delivery charges (usually $35 to $50) and control delivery times by hauling landscape materials yourself in a pickup or trailer. The yard workers at the supply center will load your vehicle free of charge with a front-end loader or skid loader. Do not overload your vehicle. Although most operators are aware of load limits, they will typically put in as much as you tell them to. As a general rule of thumb, a compact truck (roughly the size of a Ford Ranger) can handle one scoop of dirt, sand or gravel, which is about 3/4 of a cubic yard; a half-ton truck (Ford F-150) will take a scoop and a half (a little over a cubic yard), and a three-quarter ton truck (F-250) can haul two scoops (one and a half cubic yards) safely. Be sure to check the gross vehicle weight and payload data label on the driver's door.

Artificial Stone

Beyond natural stone and pavers is an entire subgroup of stone products that are manmade. Artificial stone, such as the popular brand Coronado, has the look and texture of natural stone. In fact, molds for this particular product are created from hand-selected natural stones; but the "rock" is formed from mixing pieces off aggregate, cement, and iron oxide pigments. Generally, the formula is poured into a mold that vibrates to produce realistic textures, wear, and tear. The result is an extremely lightweight veneer product (4 to 12 pounds per square foot) that is about half the cost of natural stone and readily available. You can purchase concrete stone veneer, as the products are called, at large home centers.

Why go faux? For one, the extensive variety of surface treatments effectively mimics what you'll find in the natural stone category. You'll find ledgestone, ashlar, and rubble with dimples, ripples, jagged edges, rounded rims—anything you want. You can search online for "manmade stone veneer" or "cultured stone" and find a slew of manufacturers that produce the look-alikes. Ask a professional installer for recommendations, or consult with an experienced DIYer who has worked with the product to get a review before purchasing a load for your project.

You'll have an easier time transporting and lifting manmade stone because of its contents. Cement weighs less than natural stone. Much less. The bonus of using a lighter-weight product is less poundage, which means less foundation preparation. Also, the product is easy to manipulate. You can cut it just as you would natural stone, using a masonry blade, circular masonry saw, hatchet, or wide-tooth nipper.

Many stones are colored so they contain shade variations that make them look more natural. Regarding color fastness, any stone—manmade or extracted from the earth—will fade and wear when exposed to the elements. However, iron oxide colorant is blended into the cement mix, so you could say that the color runs deep in many products. But be sure to ask. Not all products are colored all the way through. This is especially important to keep in mind if you will be cutting the stones to fit them into a particular pattern. You could end up exposing a cement core and ruining the appeal of your project.

There are several applications for cultured stone. These days, when you see a home with stone siding or accents, the surface is likely manmade. The product has interior applications on walls and floors, and for fireplace surrounds. Outdoors, it is used as siding or applied on

MANMADE RETAINING BLOCK WALLS are available in sizes and shapes that easily form angles and curved surfaces.

stucco walls. In the landscape, you can purchase pavers made from cultured stone. You can purchase irregular riverstones and randomly place them in a patio design (they aren't so random because they are meant to fit together like a puzzle—just one that looks unintentional). You'll also find tumbled cobblestones and a selection of pavers that are easy to install.

Why might you decide to forgo faux and choose natural stone for your project instead? Proper installation is the key to mimicking a real stone look. When using manmade stone veneer as facing for a wall, you must be careful not to leave gaps between stones or uneven joints. The stones are not nearly as thick as natural stone. Finally, though manmade products are created to look like the real deal, they aren't. Natural stone enthusiasts won't be fooled.

VENEER STONE has a refined, timeless appearance that is a very convincing imitation of the real thing. Because the manmade product is much lighter in weight than natural stone and is engineered for ease of installation, it is a very practical solution for siding your home.

VENEER STONE can be used to side your whole house, one or two walls, or even just one or two partial walls. In fact, it often has the most effective design impact when it is used in conjunction with other siding products, such as the lap siding seen here.

A SAMPLING of manufactured stone colors and shapes. Some styles are sold in individual units and others come in prefabricated panels that are attached to the exterior wall sheathing.

Interlocking Blocks & Pavers

Today's concrete pavers and interlocking blocks are a significant departure from the monotone surfaces previously associated with these cast concrete products. Those perfect squares and pre-formed "stones" with their contrived colors fought against the natural environment in much the same way as a new strip mall encroaches on the charm of a quaint cobbled main street. Still, they were useful and functional, for the most part providing everything required of surface paving material—if one was satisfied with the sparkly, geometric newness of it.

Now, erase that picture from your memory. The reputation of concrete pavers and interlocking blocks has changed entirely with the vast color selection, tumbled-and-treated products, selection in shapes and sizes, and sheer availability of the product. You won't run out of options in the style department. Pavers and blocks are segmental surfaces. Rather than pouring concrete, you piece them together to achieve a desired pattern. You can bet on their uniformity, which can relieve design headaches. Depending on the style and paver size you choose, you can recreate the look of a weathered piazza or an office supply superstore, if that's your preference.

Another attractive point: Pavers are relatively eco-friendly. While they still require energy for production (high kiln temperatures) and raw materials are mined, they leave less of a footprint on the earth than the thick, poured concrete slabs they replace, if only by allowing runoff to drain through their gaps and into the ground instead of directing to storm sewers.

THIS CONCRETE RETAINING WALL is intended to look as though it was made from flat limestone rock. In fact, the concrete is poured into cast forms. It is pre-colored. The forms allow for a precision, interlocking design that results in a sturdy retaining wall system and easy installation.

Popular Pavers

Paver history dates back to post-World War II, when European countries such as The Netherlands and Germany began to repair damaged cobblestone streets with manufactured replacement parts, so to speak. Unlike natural cobblestones, the pavers were uniform in size, color, and a perfect match. Pavers were introduced in the U.S. market about forty years ago, though concrete slab patios were far more popular back then. The problems with concrete include frost heave, settling earth, and the resulting buckles and cracks. Pavers simply do not present this problem. They shift along with surface and sub-surface movement.

Pavers are made from mixing cement, aggregate, pigments, and dyes. The mixture is poured into molds and formed into slabs of various shapes and sizes. Some are tumbled and treated to look like old-world cobblestones. However, pavers are not cobblestones, and there is a difference between a concrete paver (cultured stone) and a stone paver. Stone pavers are actually made from minerals that are processed and reformed. Bricks are made from clay.

The landscape contracting industry has embraced pavers in the last fifteen years. The Interlocking Concrete Paver Institute (ICPI), a North American trade association for the paver industry, was founded in 1993. Since then, paver use has spread rapidly. Pavers are widely used by professional landscapers and readily available to the public at building or landscape supply stores and stoneyards.

Paver Types

You may hear of pavers generically referred to as "patio pavers" or "concrete pavers." There is a difference, depending on the raw material used to manufacture the paver. Here are the main categories of pavers you will encounter when choosing material for a path or patio.

Concrete paver: Formed chunks of concrete, available in various shapes and many colors.

Brick paver: Made from clay and fired; available in a range of red, brown, charcoal, and yellow.

Stone paver: Cut from natural stone, such as granite or sandstone; common colors fall into the blue-gray group and sandy neutrals.

Numbers tell the story of our interest in pavers as an alternative surface to natural stone. The North American paver industry has grown from 8 million square feet (8 million meters squared) in 1980 to more than 755 million square feet (75.5 million meters squared) in 2005, according to the ICPI. Globally, there is at least one square foot (0.1 meter squared) produced for every living person on earth. One thousand pavers are manufactured every second of the work day.

A QUAINT COBBLESTONE patio in a circular design is perfectly sized for a modest patio table. Consider the furniture you plan to place on your patio before breaking ground.

Selecting Pavers

Uniformity can be a beautiful thing when laying a patio or walkway. You know the exact size of each paver, and therefore can neatly plan each piece into your design, making a limited number of cuts only as necessary. Measurements are a known quantity so you can accurately estimate how much product you'll need and how those pavers will systematically fit into your design.

Pavers have the safety advantage of a nonskid surface, which is a real benefit for patio and walkway applications. With a smooth surface, you're less likely to catch a heel in the crack between pavers, and you won't have to worry about children or older adults tripping on uneven or gaping joints. Because patios and walkways are high-traffic areas, you want a surface void of hazards. With the range in colors, you won't sacrifice style for safety.

Just as with natural stone, you'll select sizes and shapes that suit the scope of the space you want to pave. Think about the colors and textures surrounding the future patio or walkway space. The idea is for the surface to blend into the environment so paths form seamless transitions from a starting point to a destination, and patios become mellow backdrops for accent plantings, water features, or even the furniture you place in the vicinity.

A palette of pavers can include variations on a color theme, so your surface will contain the gradations in color that natural stone does. You can choose different size pavers to accomplish an interesting pattern as well.

Paving Patterns

One of brick's most appreciated qualities is its adaptability to custom patterns. Shown here are some of the classics that are relatively easy to create. All are suitable for a flat surface. The diagonal bond is a nice pattern for walkways. The pinwheel design looks great with a contrasting paver in the center of each section. Circular and curved patterns often require mortar between pavers, particularly near the pattern's center. When selecting a pattern, think about color and whether you'd like a subtle mixture of tones or starkly contrasting accent bricks.

INTERLOCKING PAVERS are available in different shapes to help you accomplish the design you desire, whether a circular, herringbone, or running bond pattern.

Layout Patterns

As you consider the surface design, play with various patterns on paper. A herringbone pattern is formal and zigzag-like, ideal for masking problem areas. The running-bond pattern is a popular patio pick and useful in small areas. The basket-weave pattern is casual and easier to master than, say, a circle pattern. However, for round patios, there is no better way to create an attractive, formal setting. You can play with curves in a fan design, which is a series of arches. Want an abstract finish? Select three or four different shaped pavers and randomly place them in a mixed design. This works well for borders, as well. You can create the same effect with different sized pavers.

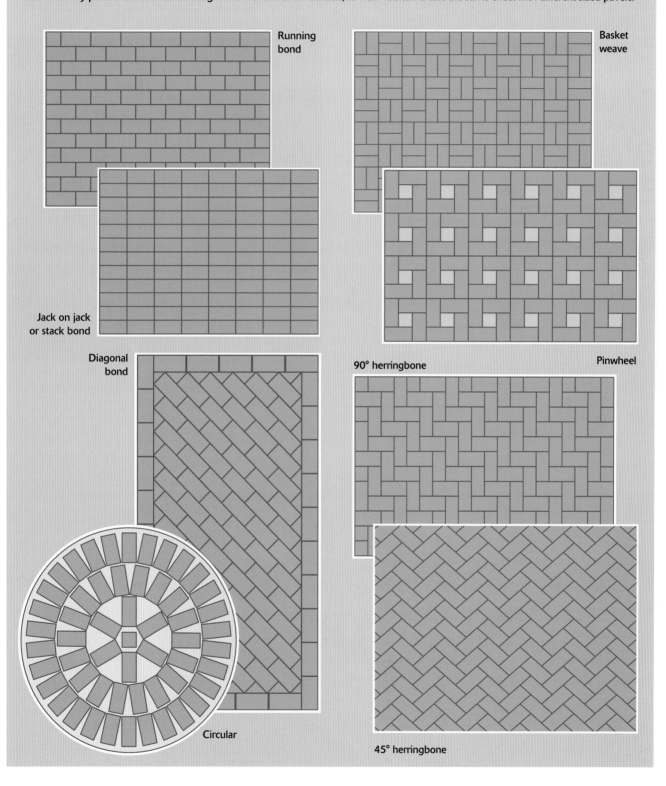

Running bond

Basket weave

Jack on jack or stack bond

Diagonal bond

90° herringbone

Pinwheel

Circular

45° herringbone

You can purchase pavers by the pallet or band, which is a fraction of a pallet. You will want to allow for extra materials, but take care to estimate the measurements of your project in advance. Many suppliers will not accept returns.

Interlocking Pavers

Interlocking pavers are modular and fit together neatly into regular shapes and patterns that may be grids or curves. When laid properly on a bedding sand foundation, with joint sand and edging to confine the space, interlocking pavers form a sturdy, solid surface that bears heavy loads.

Permeable Pavers

Permeable interlocking concrete pavement (PICP) consists of concrete pavers separated by joints filled with small stones. Under the pavers is a layer of small stone and base bedding. When water seeps into the joints between pavers, it sinks into the stone layer, which absorbs runoff and sifts debris from storm water. Under this is an open-graded base filled with various aggregate stone from ¼ inch (6 mm) to 3 inches (75 mm). Together, these layers make the surface water-permeable. PICP is considered sustainable by the U.S. Green Building Council because it limits water pollution and reduces storm water runoff.

INTERLOCKING CONCRETE PAVERS can be used to make regular and straight grid patterns or elegantly curving patterns, depending on the type you choose and your layout strategy.

Cross-section of a PICP structure

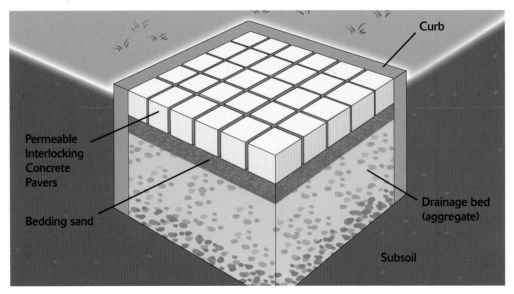

Curb

Permeable Interlocking Concrete Pavers

Bedding sand

Drainage bed (aggregate)

Subsoil

A PICP (Permeable Interlocking Concrete Pavement) is stable to walk on and also minimizes runoff into storm sewers by allowing water to pass through joints and into a drainage bed.

Interlocking Concrete Block

In a wall application, interlocking concrete blocks stack securely. The tops and bottoms of blocks are smooth and level, ideal for building a wall. Meanwhile, the facing finish may be rough and resemble natural stone. Interlocking concrete block, can weigh up to 80 pounds per block, depending on the variety you choose. This mass aids stability, but usually means the installation job will require helpers.

Retaining wall systems do not require mortar, and therefore should be used for constructing relatively low walls (less than 3 feet high). Be sure to consult the manufacturer's instructions and abide by height limits. The taller the wall, the more stabilization necessary, and you may want to enlist professional guidance. The nice thing about constructing a mortarless wall is the flexibility. As you build in a running bond pattern (see page 45 for an example), you can adjust blocks as necessary. You can purchase terrace systems and kits that contain everything you need to complete the project. The difference between interlocking block and cut stone, another option for

a dry-stacked wall, is the security of "locking" blocks together with the wall system. Some are held together with a system of overlapping flanges, and others use fiberglass pins. You can also use adhesive to secure blocks.

INTERLOCKING CONCRETE BLOCKS are used primarily for building retaining walls. They are sold in a wide assortment of shapes, sizes, and colors. Most feature a split face with a rough texture.

Fastening Methods

There are several systems for securing interlocking blocks. Depending on the system you purchase, the blocks may connect with flanges, pins, or adhesive.

OVERLAPPING FLANGES secure rows of interlocking block. The flanges automatically set the backward pitch, called the batter.

PINS DRIVE INTO cavities in the block, securing each layer of the wall.

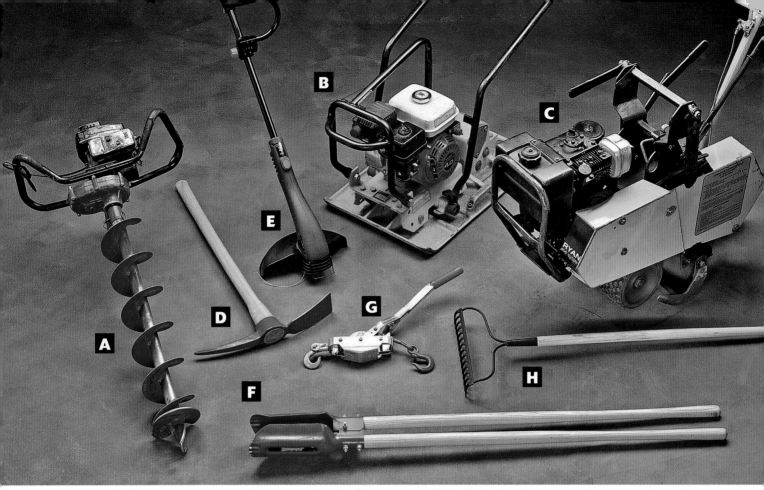

LANDSCAPING TOOLS to prepare sites for concrete projects include power auger (A) for digging holes for posts or poles; power tamper or plate compactor (B) and power sod cutter (C) for driveway and other large-scale site preparation. Smaller landscaping tools include pick (D) for excavating hard or rocky soil; weed trimmer (E) for removing brush and weeds before digging; posthole digger (F) for when you have just a few holes to dig; come-along (G) for moving large rocks and other heavy objects without excessive lifting; and garden rake (H) for moving small amounts of soil and debris.

Stonescaping Tools

A tools and materials list at the start of every project in this book will help you gather the essential equipment and supplies you'll need. Many of the required tools are everyday items that you probably have in your collection already, but other equipment is more specialized. For cutting natural stone, you won't get by without a diamond blade for your circular saw. You can always rent equipment you may not use more than once, such as a sod kicker to clear turf from a proposed patio area or a gas-powered masonry saw with a diamond blade. Inquire about rental rates and specialty equipment as you select pavers and stone.

Before you invest in tools, read consumer guides and talk to a pro at a hardware or supply store. You want sturdy, long-lasting equipment. Check grips for comfort on shovels, rakes, axes, loppers, and pruners. Be sure that the handle length is easy for you to manage tools with ease. For tools you use all the time, buy the highest quality you can afford so they last. Regarding power equipment, consider purchasing from a servicing dealer, which is like adding a professional to your team. You can take equipment to the dealership for service, purchase parts there, and always call with questions.

Working with stone is labor-intensive. You need tough tools. You'll use different shovels to transport gravel, distribute paver base, and dig edges for your patio or walkway. You'll need a quality power saw, and non-mechanical essentials like measuring tape, mason's string, and stakes.

Powerful loading equipment is helpful for moving boulders and loads of stone, pavers, or gravel. There are various classes of equipment that can take the load off moving heavy materials; you can add attachments to the same lawn tractor you use to cut the grass, or you can go all out and acquire a skid-steer loader and attachments. (You can always rent a loader if you want to use it on a per project basis.) A skid-steer loader is versatile and compact. You can add a box blade attachment for grading land, a bucket for grabbing large specimens, or forks for lifting pallets.

Tools & Materials

Every project in this book is accompanied by a useful "Tools & Materials" list like this one so you'll know exactly what you need to get the job done. Here are a few items to familiarize yourself with:

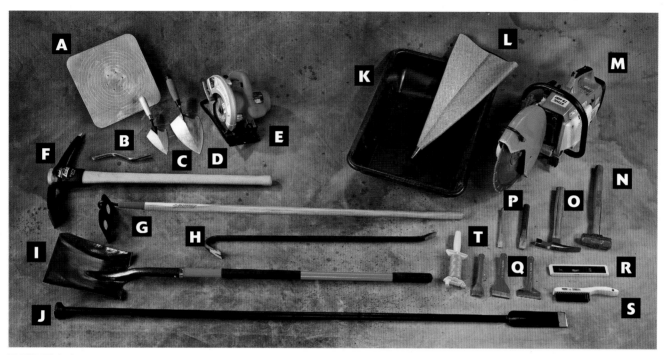

THESE TOOLS are valuable helpers when working with natural stone. Mortar hawk (A); joining tool (B); pointing trowel (C); mason's trowel (D); circular saw with masonry blade (E); pick axe (F); masonry hoe (G); wrecking bar for prying small to medium stones (H); square-end spade (I); heavy-duty spud bar for prying larger stones (J); mortar box (K); mortar bag (L); masonry saw (M); hand maul (N); brick hammer (O); stone chisels (P); bricksets (Q); torpedo level (R); wire brush (S); mason's string (T).

Safety Gear

SAFETY GEAR FOR STONEWORK includes (clockwise from top): Protective knee pads; steel-toe work boots; hard hat; eye protection; hearing protection; particle mask; sturdy gloves.

Specialty Stonescaping Tools

From left to right: A Mattock is similar to a pick axe and is used for digging or breaking up hard ground. Also called a grub hoe. **A 3-pound hand maul** can be used to crush stone, dress ragged stone edges, or drive bricksets and chisels. **Levels** are used to establish layouts and check stacked stone or masonry units. Among the more useful levels are a 4-ft. level for measuring slope san grade, a torpedo level for checking individual units, and a line level for setting layout strings.

From left to right: A wheelbarrow with at least a 5-cu.-ft. capacity is a necessity for transporting stones, loose fill, and other supplies. **A corded circular saw** with a masonry blade, preferably diamond-tipped, is used to score and cut stones and masonry units. **Landscape paint** is used to outline projects. The paint can be delivered with the can held upside down and it degrades harmlessly.

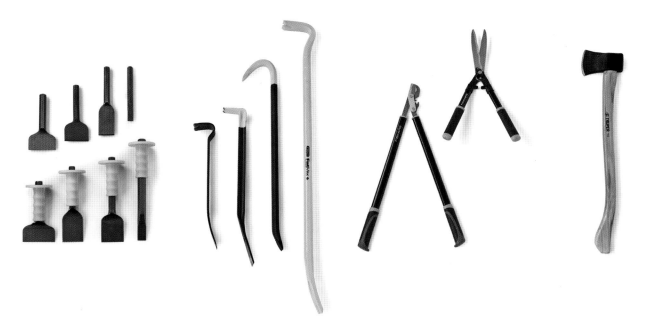

From left to right: Stone chisels and bricksets are struck with a maul to fracture or dress stones and masonry units. See pages 54 to 61. **Prybars and wrecking bars** are used to reposition larger stones. **Loppers and pruning shears** are used to trim back overgrown plants. **An axe** can be used to cut through roots in an excavation area or to cut down small tress or shrubs.

From left to right: Shovels are used for diggings and for distributing loose material. A pointed spade, a square-nose spade, and a scoop shovel are the types you'll use most. **A leaf rake** is used mostly for site cleanup. **A hand tamper** is used to compact gravel. Typical tools weigh ten pounds. **Metal pipes** are set into bedding sand to guide a wooden screed when striking off the sand.

Heavy Equipment

THIS BOX RAKE helps a land owner grade the surface.

MANY TRACTORS can support attachments, such as loaders, pallet forks, and box blades. The loader attached to this utility tractor is useful for moving heavy materials like gravel and stone.

ON A SMALLER SCALE, you'll get plenty of use out of a lawn tractor for mowing—and you can purchase attachments such as this utility cart to help haul stonescaping materials.

A TRACTOR AND BUCKET ATTACHMENT are useful when clearing and grading land to prepare for laying a patio or any hardscape surface.

A BUCKET ATTACHMENT also allows you to use a tractor to transport stone supplies and clear away debris.

A DC-POWERED WINCH mounted to a lawn tractor is a very effective piece of equipment for dragging small boulders to new locations in your yard.

Techniques for Working with Stone

Invest time in learning stone basics—how to cut it, lay it, stack it. Stonescaping is a craft. Spend the hours necessary to prepare a patio surface and measure a slope for steps. There are no short-cuts, but the outcome you will enjoy from tending to details pays off in curb appeal.

In this chapter, we walk you through techniques to manipulate stone—how to work it and how to work with it. You will have a flashback to geometry class with figures for plotting out steps. We'll talk about ways you can safely lift and move stone as you work. And we'll review cutting basics so you are prepared to shape stone to fit your design. Study these sections and refer to them as you take on the projects in this book. Whatever your stonescaping project may be, you will almost certainly need to employ one or all of these techniques to get the job done.

BREAKING STONE is a simple process but it requires a lot of practice to be done well. A stone chisel, a maul and a soft surface are the primary tools you'll need.

Handling Stone

Natural stone is about as organic a material as you will find. When selecting it you will encounter unlimited variations in shape, interesting bumps and grooves, and textural beauty marks. No two natural stones are exactly the same. However, the characteristics that make natural stone so appealing for landscape can create challenges when trying to build a uniform structure like a wall. If you choose natural stone over manufactured block, cutting and shaping is just part of the job. So is lifting and positioning, which isn't easy when working with large boulders.

Don't be intimidated by the process. You can manipulate stone just as you would prune a shrub; though your plants obviously don't require the use of a mallet and chisel, and your stones are not likely to grow back. Take your time and study the steps for cutting and shaping stone.

Cutting Tools

Designate an area for cutting and shaping, preferably a grassy spot that will absorb the shock of heavy tools striking stone. This is your "cutting zone." It is important to keep children out of the dangerous area where stone chips could fly. You may use sandbags to anchor rounded stones while cutting. Or, you can build a banker to absorb shock (see below). A banker resembles a small sandbox, and you construct it with two layers of stacked 2 × 2s, forming a frame. Sandwich a piece of ¾"-thick plywood between the two layers. Pour sand on top of the plywood. You can set stone in the sand while cutting and shaping. If you prefer to stand while cutting, build up your banker by laying a foundation of stacked concrete block.

A BANKER is a sand-filled wood box that provides a shock-absorbent surface for cutting stone.

Lifting & Moving Stone

Many of the projects in this book require large, heavy stones. Even small stones can cause injury to your back if you don't lift and move them properly. Always support your back with lifting belts. You're doing some heavy lifting yourself, and it warrants use of this support-wear. Gloves are a good idea, too. Always bend at your knees when you lift stone. If you can't straighten up, the stone is too heavy to lift by yourself.

Other helpful stone-moving tools are ramps and simple towing devices, such as chains. When stacking interlocking block to construct a retaining wall, you may need a "helper" to lift stones as you build up some height. You can use 2 x 4s as ramps, placing a couple of them side-by-side to accommodate larger blocks. Using stone as a support underneath a ramp (2 x 4s), angle the ramp from the ground to the retaining wall. From a squatting position, push the stone up the ramp using your knees, not your back. You can also use a come-along tool (see page 48) to drag heavy stones.

Always add at least 10 percent to your materials estimate when ordering stone. That way, you can practice cutting and "dressing" skills, and you will allow for unavoidable waste that occurs from miscuts and routine trimming.

Now that your cutting surface is in order, collect all necessary tools and materials. The type of stone will dictate this. Always wear protective goggles and gloves while cutting, and if you are creating dust wear a nuisance-rated particle mask (using wet-cutting techniques is a good way to limit the dust.)

Cutting stone calls for heavy-duty tools: a pitching chisel for long clean cuts; a pointing chisel for removing small bumps; a basic stone chisel; a sturdy maul; a sledgehammer; and a mason's hammer, which has a pick at one end that is helpful for breaking off small chips. For a circular saw, use a masonry blade (preferrably diamond-tipped) designed for the material you are cutting. Hard material like marble and concrete will require a different blade than softer stones like flagstone and limestone. Along with the hardware, you'll need a pipe or 2 × 4 for cutting flagstone. Also, keep on hand chalk or a crayon for marking cut lines.

A POINTING CHISEL is used to clean up edges and surfaces by knocking off small chunks and ridges.

A PITCHING CHISEL has a relatively wide blade for making long, clean cuts.

A BASIC STONE CHISEL can handle a variety of stonecutting tasks, including cleaving stones in two.

Cutting & Shaping

You can dress a stone, which is to polish it by removing rough edges and chipping off bumps and ridges. Or, you can make clean cuts by scoring and splitting stone. Which technique you choose should depend on the shape, thickness, and size of the stone. Regardless of the type of cut, always remove the stone from its setting when working it. Do not be tempted to dress a stone that is already positioned in a retaining wall—even if all you intend to do is chip away a few bumps. You could damage surrounding stones and break the mortar bond. Remember, you have a "cutting zone" for this type of work—use it.

Essential Cuts

A basic dressing cut calls for a chisel and mallet. Point the chisel at a 30- to 45-degree angle at the base of the piece you wish to remove. Tap the maul lightly, gradually working a break line. Think of this as connect-the-dots. You'll then use your chisel and mallet to forcefully chip off the piece. Or, you can rely on the pick end of your masonry hammer to chip away pieces. The goal of "dressing" stone is to refine the shape, even out rough spots, and also to clean up after major cuts.

DRESSING A STONE involves chipping off small irregularities to improve the surface.

How to Cut Stone with a Stone Chisel

1 Draw a cutting line with chalk and then lightly score along the line with a stone chisel and maul.

2 Strike with a stone chisel along the scored cutting line until the stone fractures—hopefully along the line.

Cut flagstone by using the basic cut method. Flagstone pieces can be quite large. For the best control, cut small sections at a time, marking cut lines with chalk. Examine the rock for fissures and places where it will naturally break. Ideally, your cut lines will fall in place with these fissures, making the job easier for you. After marking flagstone, score it by moving the chisel along the cut line and striking it with the maul. (Again, think connect-the-dots.) Now, flip the flagstone over and place it on a 2 × 4 or pipe. Your score mark should line up with the edge of the 2 × 4 or pipe. The area to be removed is propped up. Strike this area with the maul, and the fieldstone will break apart along the scored line you created.

1 Trying to split a large flagstone in half can lead to many unpredicted breaks. For best results, chip off small sections at a time. Mark the stone on both sides with chalk or a crayon, indicating where you want it to split. If there is a fissure nearby, mark your line there since that is probably where the stone will break naturally.

2 Score along the line on the back side of the stone (the side that won't be exposed) by moving a chisel along the line and striking it with moderate blows with a maul. Option: If you have a lot of cutting to do, reduce hammering fatigue by using a circular saw to score the stones, and a maul and chisel to split them. Keep the stone wet during cutting with a circular saw to reduce dust.

3 Turn the stone over, place a pipe or 2 × 4 directly under the chalk line, then strike forcefully with the maul on the end of the portion to be removed.

Fieldstone cuts require using sandbags or a banker to brace the stone. Because of its rounded surface, the rock will shift and roll during the cutting process, which is a safety hazard. Mark the cut line with chalk or a crayon, examining the rock for natural fissures. Score with the chisel and maul, then strike along the score line with a pitching chisel to split the stone.

Ashlar, or wall stones, should be flat on the top and bottom and resemble a block. Sometimes you'll run across ashlar with a diagonal edge—a wing off the side that you'll want to remove to maintain the uniformity of your wall. Score a line with a small chisel and then split the jagged edge off with a pitching chisel to create a square block. You can clean up bumps and ridges with the pick end of a mason's hammer.

Pitching chisel

USE A PITCHING CHISEL to dress jagged edges on ashlar and other cut stones so you can stack them more effectively.

How to Cut Fieldstone

PLACE THE STONE ON A BANKER, or prop it with sandbags, and mark with chalk or a crayon all the way around the stone, indicating where you want it to split. If possible, use the natural fissures in the stone as cutting lines.

SCORE ALONG THE LINE using moderate blows with a chisel and maul, then strike solidly along the score line with a pitching chisel to split the stone. Dress the stone with a pointing chisel.

Circular Saw Technique

A CIRCULAR SAW FITTED WITH A MASONRY BLADE made of bonded abrasive is used to score breaking lines into stones. Lay a piece of thin plywood on the rock to protect the foot of the saw. Douse the stone with water periodically to prevent overheating and limit dust.

If you are cutting a lot of thick stone, avoid fatigue while increasing control by using a circular saw. Install a toothless masonry blade (bonded abrasive, preferably diamond coated or tipped). Always wear safety gear (goggles, gloves, dust mask), and keep children away from your cutting area. The goal is to make a deep score line for cutting, not to cut all the way through. Set the depth of cut on your saw to $\frac{1}{8}$" (3 mm) and score a line in three passes, increasing the cutting depth by $\frac{1}{8}$" for each pass. Flip the stone and score a line that's aligned with the first.

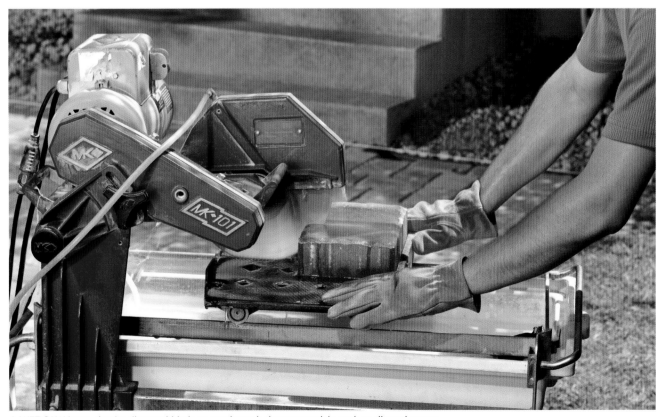

A WET SAW has a circular diamond blade to cut through dense materials, such as tile and pavers.

CREATE A SUBBASE that's stable and allows good drainage by tamping a layer of compactable gravel.

Evaluate & Measure

Surface preparation isn't something you can eyeball. You need to know your property's exact grade so you can compensate by building up a slope, or excavating land to achieve a flat plane that slopes a little for drainage. A surveyor can determine the grade of your land. Check your property plat.

Find grade with two stakes, string, a measuring tape, and a string level. Pound one stake near the foundation of your home. Tie the string to the base of this stake so it is even with the ground. Measure 10 feet (3 m) from this point and pound the second stake into the ground. Attach the string to the second stake, adjusting it as you use the level to ensure that it is level. Measure the distance between the ground and the string on the second stake. It should be at least 2 inches (5.1 cm) for paved surfaces and 6 inches (15.2 cm) or more for lawns and mulch. A 10-foot (3-m) distance with a 6-inch distance has a 5-percent grade, which is ideal.

Prepping the Foundation

The foundation you prepare for a patio, walkway, or retaining wall will determine the stability of the surface. You need sound infrastructure, which means proper drainage and flat ground—a compact layer on which to lay natural stone or pavers. The real work in most projects is invested beneath the surface. (The gratifying steps are topping your foundation prep with beautiful stone.) Most of our yards have soggy spots, dips, and slopes that need mending. We'll walk through the steps so you can set the foundation for a stone/paver surface that will last.

TIE A MASON'S LINE TO A STAKE at the high point of your yard and then extend the string out to the low point. Level the line, then measure from the line down to the ground at various points to determine the overall slope, and to identify high and low spots that will need to be excavated or filled.

Estimate the gravel and sand you will need to complete the gravel foundation with these simple formulas:

Gravel: For a 4" (10.2 cm) layer of gravel, surface area (square feet) divided by 50 equals the tons needed (cubic meters times 2.4 equals metric equivalent). Equation: SA / 50 = tons needed

Sand: For sand, surface area divided by 100 equals the tons needed (cubic meters times 1.6 equals metric equivalent). Equation: SA / 100 = tons needed.

Examine the topography of your property. Are there ruts or sink holes in the area where you will install your project? Do you notice places where water collects? Are there tree roots, bushes, or other plants that you must remove? With paper and a pencil, sketch a rough diagram of your backyard, drawing in the position of your new stonescape project.

Outline the project. Reach for your measuring tape, several landscape stakes (enough to create at least four corners), string, and line level. Drive stakes into the ground well beyond the perimeter of the space you will excavate to lay the foundation. You don't want to have to move these stakes once you start digging. Tie string

connecting the stakes about 4 inches (10.2 cm) from the grade, creating a ring around your project. Using a line level, adjust string so it is perfectly level, as described earlier. Now, move down the string on the stakes farthest from the house to create a ¾-inch (6-mm) per foot drainage pitch.

To outline a curved patio or walkway, lay a garden hose in the ground to "draw" the shape. For even circles, make a large compass by tying a string to a stake and tying the other end of the string to a can of spray paint. Pull the string taut and spray the ground as you walk around the circle. Set some stakes and string around the circle shape to pitch your project away from the house before you start digging.

OUTLINE THE PROJECT AREA using stakes and mason's string to find a layout you like and to measure the existing grade.

TO MARK A CIRCLE, tie a string to a can of landscape spray paint, measure along the string the distance of the curve radius and tie the other end of the string to a stake driven at that point. Pull the string taut and spray paint the curve onto the ground.

How to Prepare a Compactable Gravel Base

A layer of compactable gravel can be tamped down to create a very sturdy subbase for building on, while still allowing drainage. You can add a layer of coarse sand on top to create a perfect bed for setting pavers or flagstones. A power tamper (also called a plate compactor) is helpful for compacting gravel before laying pavers. You can rent this equipment from a hardware store or landscape retailer.

BE THOROUGH WHEN TAMPING down compactable gravel. When you're finished, the surface should feel nearly as stable and skid-free as concrete

1. **Lay out and dig the base.** Lay a base that is at least 6" (15.2 cm) deeper than the thickness of your stone or pavers. Establish reference points for taking depth measurements using grade stakes and string. Use string to create intersecting lines that cross your project area, tying a piece of string every 4 ft. Lines should almost, but not quite, touch the perimeter lines you set earlier. Drive stakes at the end of each string line. Mark on the stakes where the surface of the project must be.

2. **Using a shovel, remove soil from the area.** (Account for the thickness of the paver, plus 5" [12.7 cm].) Excavate 8" (20.3 cm) beyond the edge of your project. After removing soil, pull out the stakes and strings and then lay a straight 2 × 4 in the excavated space, placing a level on top to double-check whether the slope.

   Add and compact the base material. Spread a layer of compactable gravel (paver base or class V) in the excavated area. The base should fill the excavated area, leaving space for the thickness of your pavers plus ½ in. (1.3 cm). For example, if your pavers are 1" thick (2.5 cm), your excavated area should be 6" (15.2 cm) deep, and you should fill the excavation with 4½" (11.4 cm) of paver base (after compaction).

3. **Once the paver base is even** and the correct slope is established, flatten the area with a plate compactor. Check for flatness and pitch with your 2 × 4 and level.

4. **Install edging.** Edging should be level with the patio or walkway surface so it does not look like an add-on that sticks out. Paver edging is sometimes confused with landscape edging, but they are very different products. Paver edging sits firmly on the base and snaps together in units. You drive galvanized metal spikes through the edging into the paver base to secure the border. Natural flagstone does not require paver edging.

5. **Spread sand.** Before spreading sand, lay 1" (2.5-cm) outside-diameter pipes or wood strips over the paver base, spaced every 6 ft. (1.8 m). These are depth spacers called screed guides for your sand base. Spread sand by running your 2 × 4 along the screed guides, smoothing low piles of sand level with the guides. The tops of the paver edge sections must be higher than the sand level, so they cannot be used as screed guides. Once the sand is leveled, remove the guides and fill in the grooves left behind with sand. Now, you are ready to lay pavers.

1 Transfer the height mark from each string intersection point to a wood stake at the point of intersection. Measure down and mark slope lines on the stakes.

Landscape fabric is not necessary underneath a paver patio, but if you do lay it down, install fabric before filling in the excavated area with paver base. Landscape fabric is best in applications where weed growth may present a problem, such as under loose fill gravel in a Zen garden or pathway. In those cases, be sure to integrate the fabric with solid edging. In a patio application, the paver base layer acts as a weed barrier.

2 Excavate the site using the strings and stakes as a reference for how deep you need to dig. After the soil is removed, add a layer of compactable gravel and smooth it out with a 2 × 4.

3 Test the grade of the base after you have compacted the gravel with a plate compactor or a hand tamper. Use a long level or a smaller level on top of a long 2 × 4 to make sure the slope is consistent.

4 Paver edge is a rigid plastic edging material that is secured to the ground with spikes. The vertical flange is buttressed for greater strength. It provides a much more stable border than plastic landscape edging.

Screed guide

5 Lay metal pipes in the sand base to create screed guides that will support a 2 × 4 screed board while you level the sand to a consistent depth.

Laying Pavers & Stone

Whenever you sand-set a paver or piece of natural stone (such as flagstone), you are filling an excavated void with a functional, pleasing surface that will become part of a pathway or patio. A pathway, in turn, will usher visitors through your yard. A patio will serve as an entertainment hub. It is a great benefit of both of these features that they can be created with no permanent bonding agents or fasteners. You simple set the paver or stone into a sand base and you're basically done.

Take care when setting pavers and stones. Scrutinize places where stones should be cut to fit and make sure you're getting it right. Your detail-oriented handiwork will result in a neat, professional job. Sloppy corners and uneven joints will spoil all your hard work in preparing for the surface. When working with pavers, most have self-spacing lugs, which automatically separate the pavers for joints. Press two units together, side by side, and the lugs will meet. Do not shuffle pavers sideways in the sand. Do not try to tap the pavers level. The plate compactor will level them later. As you approach the edges, measure and set the remaining pieces of paver edge. Scrape away the sand and set the edging directly on the paver base. Partly set the spikes so you can move the edging if needed. When setting a flagstone walkway or patio, you may also opt for a free-flowing approach to laying stone. Piece together the surface much like you would put together a puzzle, cutting and shaping stone when necessary.

CONCRETE PAVERS are set directly onto a stable bed of sand one at a time and then tamped down as a group to become flat, level and firmly seated.

BROAD, FLAT PAVING STONES like flagstone must be set and adjusted individually to account for differences in thickness and unevenness on the bottoms.

After setting natural flagstones, use a level or 2×4 to ensure the surface is flat. Adjust uneven units by adding or removing sand beneath them. Take your time and work methodically through the process of examining your work, making adjustments, and checking for evenness.

You'll finish the surface by sweeping sand over the patio or walkway surface and into the joints. With manufactured pavers, use a plate compactor to level the pavers and work sand into joints. Continue sweeping and plate compacting until the joints do not accept more sand.

PAVERS THAT ARE TOO HIGH can be identified by dragging a flat 2×4 across the surface. Often, a high paver can be lowered simply by rapping it with a rubber mallet. If that doesn't work, remove the paver and scrape out some of the sand.

SWEEP GRANULAR FILL into the gaps between pavers to lock the individual units in place. Refresh the fill occasionally as the level goes down.

FOR A MORE FORMAL LOOK, fill gaps between pavers with premixed sand that contains a hardening agent. After moistening, tool the joints with a masonry jointing tool.

Building with Stone

Fieldstone walls that snake through the countryside have a charming, tumbled appearance that makes you think they must have been thrown together casually. But their longevity tells a different story. Stone, when properly stacked and skillfully set, will weather the ages. The techniques we employ today when assembling a dry stacked wall or mortaring layers of stone have not changed over the years. However, today's products and the conveniences they offer certainly ease the process. Interlocking blocks exempt the do-it-yourselfer from cutting and shaping stone; the blocks fit together almost automatically and form sturdy structures. Natural stone walls of ashlar or flagstone require a bit more artistry and puzzle-solving to secure each layer, but the selection of stone available at stoneyards includes cuts that are designed to be used in wallbuilding with no (or very little) on-site cutting.

Whether you choose to fill gaps with mortar for a more secure structure, or to dry stack a wall to achieve an organic look, building a wall requires a methodical approach.

MORTARED STONE WALLS have a more permanent appearance than dry-laid walls, but if they are not built on a sturdy concrete footing the shifting that occurs will cause the mortar joints to fail quickly.

Mortar or Dry Stack?

Mortar walls are sturdy and you won't find plants peeking through the cracks. (This can be good or bad, depending on whether you prefer a completely polished look or a more natural finish.) You'll also see it in walls that use rounded stones and veneers, which are polished face stones embedded in walls for appearance only.

There are many advantages to interlocking walls, which do not require mortar for sticking power. You can set them on a flexible, crushed gravel base, and drainage is not generally a problem, as water can bleed through the stacked stones' crevices. Dry stacked walls blend with other landscape features and the natural environment; they are far less "uptight" than a mortared wall. Ultimately, your choice to construct a mortar or interlocking wall will depend on the style of your home and your preference for manicured vs. natural landscapes.

DRY-SET STONE WALLS are made by stacking stones and relying solely on gravity and the natural shapes of the stones to hold them together. The exception is the top row of flat stones, called the cap stones, that should be bonded to the course below with mortar or masonry adhesive.

All About Mortar

Mortar is like batter. You must measure ingredients carefully and mix it according to the instructions, otherwise the result will be a flop. Mortar that is too dry crumbles, is hard to spread and does not have enough initial tack to cling to the stone surfaces properly. If you add too much water, mortar is messy, diluted, and weak.

While following the manufacturer's mixing instructions—which should be interpreted as guidelines—gradually add water, starting with three-quarters of the recommended amount. You may use less or more water to create a mixture that clings to the trowel and spreads easily, like frosting. You'll want to mix mortar in batches so it does not harden before you've applied it. You can add water to thickened mortar (called retempering), but you must use this doctored substance within two hours. Adding a latex bonding agent (also called acrylic fortifier) increases the plasticity of the mortar and makes it easier to spread.

The best container for mixing mortar is a mortar box, and the best tool for applying it is a pointed trowel. To mix mortar, dump the dry mortar mix into the mortar box (don't mix more than you can use in 20 minutes or so) and make a depression in the center of the pile. Pour water into this depression. Blend with a masonry hoe, taking your time and observing consistency. You can always add more water, but if you've already emptied the bag of dry mix, you're out of luck if your mixture is soupy.

You'll need a surface to work mortar. A temporary table consisting of concrete blocks and a plywood top will suffice. Pour mixed mortar on to the surface, then shape it into a loaf. Using your trowel, slice off a strip of mortar, enough to spread across three bricks. (Note: If you are laying ashlar stone, you will cover less surface area in a single swipe because each stone contains more surface area.) "Throw" the mortar by smearing it across the surface in a single swipe. Then, drag the point of the trowel through the center of the mortar, called furrowing. This distributes mortar evenly. Repeat the process: throw and furrow, throw and furrow. Lay stone or brick on the freshly mortared surface, working in small sections so it does not dry.

TO MIX MORTAR, empty as much dry mix as you need into a mortar box and create a depression in the center. Add water in the depression and blend with a masonry hoe.

TRANSFER THE MORTAR, which should have the consistency of frosting, to a hawk (here, a scrap of plywood) and load your trowel.

FLICK THE TROWEL to dislodge any loosely hanging mortar so it does not fall off in transit and then place the mortar on your project stones.

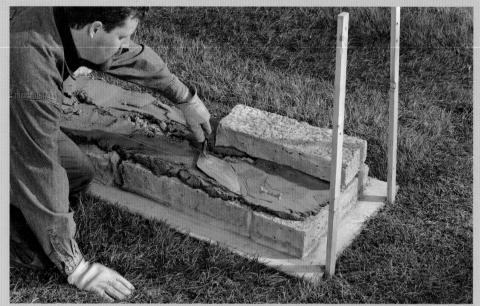

A MORTAR BED is laid to bond stones to a concrete footing. When working with flat stones, lay a mortar bed on top of each new course. If you are mortaring fieldstones, it often works better to apply the mortar directly to each stone and set it into position (called buttering).

Footings

Check local building codes before constructing a retaining wall or any other major landscape structure. Footings are required for most concrete, stone, brick, and block structures that adjoin with other permanent structures and exceed code height limits. Footings provide a sturdy, level base that stabilizes brick, block, and poured concrete structures. If you opt for a mortared wall, you must create a concrete footing. (By filling the joints, you create a "permanent" structure that must meet code.) Footings for dry stacked walls are less involved. A crushed gravel base will provide appropriate stability and drainage.

Concrete footings should be twice as wide as the wall they will support and extend 12 inches (30.5 cm) past the ends of the wall. The footing must extend below the frost line in cold climates. Anchoring the base below this line will prevent the footing from shifting as the soil freezes and thaws. The retaining wall project in this book uses a dry stack method, freeing you from the obligation of building a concrete footing. The labor involved in establishing this base may help you decide whether to construct a mortared or dry stacked wall in the first place.

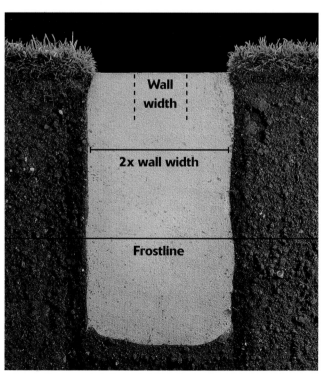

A CONCRETE FOOTING should extend down past the frostline (the shallowest depth that never freezes in winter). The footing should be twice as wide as the wall.

Wall Components

Tie stones: These long stones span the entire width of your structure (or at least two-thirds of it), tying together the faces of walls that are two or more stones thick and improving wall strength.

Ashlar stone: Blocky cuts of stone come in different varieties and are rectangular in shape for easy stacking.

Fieldstone: Rounded stones are best for the lower parts of walls and offer a rustic look.

Rubble: This is ideal for filling gaps between outer faces (called wythes) of a fieldstone wall.

Capstone: Smooth, uniform flat stones placed on top of a wall to give it a polished look and protect the interior from water infiltration.

Interlocking block: Generally made from light concrete and aggregate, which is a composed of sand, various stone, and other minerals, interlocking blocks fit together snugly and do not require mortar. They are available in various styles and sizes.

USE A BATTER GAUGE and level as you lay stone walls, which should angle inwards or get thinner as they get taller. Freestanding walls made of ashlar should have a batter of 1" for every 2 ft. of height. Retaining walls and fieldstone walls should have a batter of 1" per foot.

Capstone

Tie stone

Tie stone

TIE STONES ARE CRITICAL to the sturdiness of a wall, especially if it is dry-stacked. These stones are long enough to span all the way from the front to the back of the wall. As a general rule of thumb, at least 20% of the stones in a wall should be tie stones that are spaced around evenly.

INTERLOCKING BLOCKS are cast from concrete and used primarily in retaining walls. Some are cast with flanges that lock individual blocks together, while others are held together with pins or masonry adhesive.

Dry Stacked Walls

Interlocking block is virtually fool-proof for constructing dry-stacked retaining walls and low garden walls. You can purchase a variety of styles, including "tumbled" blocks that have faces more closely resembling natural, weathered stone. Different shapes and sizes allow you to create curved surfaces with ease. Interlocking blocks designed for larger walls have flanges and niches so they can lock together (thus the name). Lip-and-groove style blocks connect at the bottom. Some styles have holes at the top and bottom of blocks so you can attach vertical layers. Pins driven into these holes secure the blocks in place. As you explore the design possibilities, you may consider bringing on a professional who can assist.

The natural alternative to interlocking block is ashlar, which can include limestone and other stones depending on your region. While ashlar does not offer the handy nooks and grooves that assure a perfect fit, its blocky and fairly consistent rectangular shape is ideal for stacking.

Stacking natural stone requires a bit of mixing and matching. You'll want to lay out stones on the ground and examine their different shapes and sizes. They will vary, even if slightly. Separate the stones that will require cutting or shaping (refer to previous chapter). Natural stone is not uniform like interlocking block. You must

"ASHLAR" REFERS TO any stone that is cut into a shape with square corners and flat surfaces. These are used mostly for building natural stone walls.

compensate for thinner stones and stagger vertical joints to improve stability. Shims, which are thin slivers of angled rock, can be used to fill gaps by raising stones. Stack thinner stones to equal the thickness of sturdier stones. For instance, three slimmer ashlar stones may match the height of a single adjacent stone.

Dry laid walls consist of two wythes or layers of stacked stone that lean together slightly. You'll prepare a 6-inch (15.2-cm) deep base that extends 6 inches. beyond the wall on all sides. Form a V shape in this base so gravel in the center is 2 inches (5.1 cm) lower than the edges. As you stack the two sides of stone and build up some height, use a batter gauge and level to ensure that the side angles inward.

A WYTHE is a row of stones that runs the full length of the wall horizontally. For stability, stone walls should be built with at least two wythes that lean against one another in the center for support. Voids between stones and between wythes can be filled with small chunks of filler stone.

STONE THICKNESS VARIES, even with ashlar. In many cases, this can be managed by stacking two or three thinner stones next to a thick stone to obtain equal heights.

FIELDSTONE AND OTHER ROUND STONES, such as river rock, are tougher to dry-stack than ashlar, but it is certainly a manageable job. Stacking fieldstone into low walls is a traditional way to deal with stones when clearing fields for planting or grazing.

THIN FLAT STONES called cap stones are set into mortar beds or adhesive to top off most dry-stack walls. The mortar beds should be between ½" and 1" thick.

DESIGNING STEPS requires some math work. You'll need to figure out the total rise and run of the project and then calculate the best size for each step.

Construction Details

While the labor of creating projects from stone is physically demanding, there is quite a bit of headwork involved as well. From prepping a patio foundation to mixing mortar and taking precise measurements for steps, you'll sharpen your math skills as you embark on the endeavors in this book. You must be precise. Going back to the old input-output idea, your project results will reflect whether you dedicated the time to "figure it out" before digging in to the steps. Here, we rehash a few geometry lessons—rise, run, and slope. You'll learn how to put them to work while building steps and prepping

a retaining wall base that successfully addresses drainage issues.

Conquering Steps

Outdoor steps, like the timber and gravel garden steps in this book (see pages 90 to 95), consist of treads and risers. Outside, the earth serves as the "stringer," supporting treads and risers. (In a home, the stringer is that saw-tooth escalating frame that holds treads and risers.) The tread is the area you step on. The depth of the step can be several feet if you are scaling a long sloped backyard. The riser is the vertical support, or lift, that takes you to the next level.

Steps should have uniform rise and run for safety reasons—you don't want people to trip and fall—and for pure function. You want stairs to be even, and they're more attractive that way. Building steps require a bit of preliminary math. First, you must determine the rise and run of the slope. Use landscape stakes to mark beginning and ending points of the slope: the top and bottom. Then, run a level, horizontal string line, or board from the high stake to the low stake. Measure the vertical and horizontal distances the slope covers. When figuring measurements for steps, you must determine the unit rise and run, and total rise and run. The unit rise and run of each step will have the same ratio as the total rise and run of the slope. How many steps you choose to make is determined by your materials and the formula below.

Rise & Run Math

In outdoor settings, most people comfortably step on treads that are 18 inches (61 cm) deep and 4 inches (10.2 cm) high. This amount of space doesn't require adjusting one's natural stepping pattern to reach the next level. If you choose to create longer treads for steps that gradually scale up a shallow slope, exaggerate the depth so people can take two or three steps before hitting that next riser. Avoid uncomfortable in-between depths that force walkers to stretch rather than naturally climb to the next level.

Comfortable at Any Slope

Generations of experience have provided landscapers with a reliable formula for step rise and run: $(2 \times \text{rise}) + \text{run} = 26"$. Low steps have long runs because you can take a longer step if you have to raise your foot as high. Taller steps need shorter runs for the opposite reason. That said, you can match your steps to any slope and still have them be comfortable. You probably will not match your slope exactly using the formula below, but get as close as you can. Then adjust your tread length as needed. Be sure to adjust all treads by the same amount.

Table 1.

Riser height (in inches)	From*	Best run (in inches) (total tread length)**
3.5	Actual width of 4 × 6	19
4		18
5		16
5.5	Actual width of 6 × 6	15
6		14
7	Width of railroad tie***	12
7.5	Width of 8 × 8	11

* Figures based on typical dimensions of commonly available timbers.
** Run based on average step-stride capacity given in the outdoor step formula: $(2 \times \text{rise}) + \text{run} = 26"$.
*** Typical railroad tie is 7 × 9".

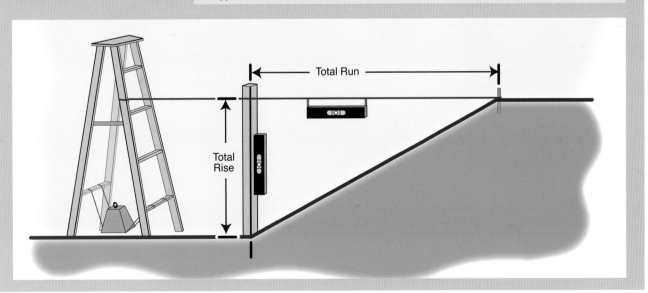

Retaining Wall Parameters

We discussed freestanding wall techniques in the previous chapter, noting dry and mortar laying processes and how to choose appropriate stone material. Retaining walls are only visible from one side; the back is flush against the grade and must withstand pressure from soil, especially when that soil gains even more poundage under wet conditions. With this in mind, larger retaining walls rely on behind-the-scenes elements like drain tile and gravel backfill for proper drainage and overall stability.

Examine the photo on this page. The drainage gravel behind the wall prevents soil from turning to mud and exerting pressure on the wall. Landscape fabric keeps soil from seeping into gravel, which is a sort of filter leading to the drain tile. If soil stops water from bleeding to the drain tile, you're back to the heavy-soil-mud-pressure problem. Drain tiles are installed with perforations facing down. One end of the drain tile is exposed so runoff can escape. Because dry stacked walls bleed water through their faces, drainage tile is not always necessary.

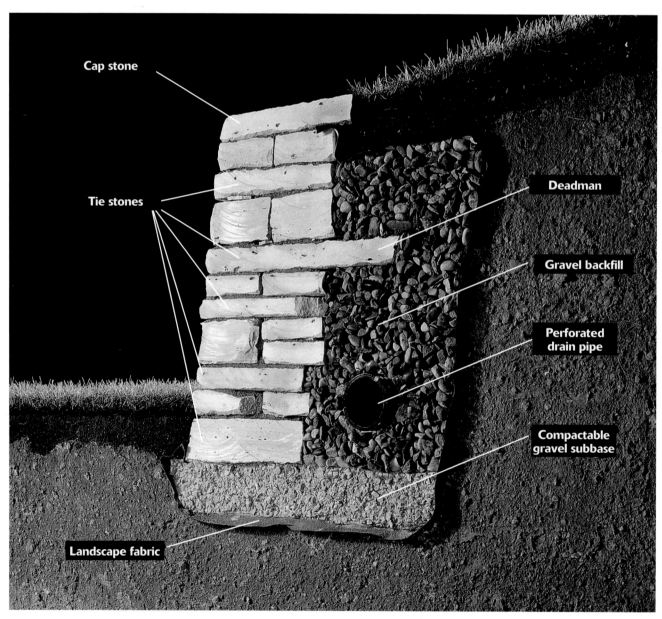

Cap stone

Tie stones

Deadman

Gravel backfill

Perforated drain pipe

Compactable gravel subbase

Landscape fabric

STONE RETAINING WALLS must contain several key design elements to allow for drainage and to hold back the pressure of the earth. "Deadmen" are long stones that are installed perpendicular to the wall and then extend back into the slope. River rock backfill creates plenty of air pockets, facilitating good drainage. To further enhance drainage, drain tile (perforated pipe) may be laid near the bottom course of the wall.

Before you dig in to a retaining wall project, check local building codes to find out if you need a permit. For walls taller than 4 feet (1.2 m), consider hiring a professional. Stone is heavy and difficult (and dangerous) to stack high without proper equipment and engineering.

Supporting the base of the wall is an 8-inch (20.3 cm) trench filled with 6 inches (15.2) of compactable gravel. Refer to leveling techniques on pages 64 to 65 as you ensure the evenness of this base layer. The first row of interlocking block will be partially embedded below the surface to enhance stability. A drain tile is installed after laying the second row of interlocking block. Pour gravel in the backfill area, place the drain tile on the gravel about 6 inches (15.2 cm) behind blocks, and continue stacking block. You'll finish off the backfill once your wall is complete by filling the space completely with gravel.

RETAINING WALLS eliminate slope problems to enhance the enjoyability of your property. One basic strategy is to build a wall that steps down at a regular pace to follow the side of a hill (left photo). Another tactic is to divide the slope into flat terraces that are contained by a series of smaller retaining walls (right photo).

Stonescaping Projects

From firepits to gravel walkways to flagstone patios, the stonescape in your landscape can feature many faces. Whether it is serene or stunning, the success of your project hinges on thoughtful preparation, careful work and a bit of well-directed brawn where needed. By applying the skills and techniques that you have seen demonstrated and described in this book, you can build virtually any backyard stonescaping project. Along with the technical advice you'll find on the pages that follows, here are some general tips to make any project go more smoothly: Hand-select your stones whenever possible so you can get exactly the material you want. Have the site preparation completed before your supplies are delivered. Arrange for plenty of help digging and lifting. And lastly, always have your utility company flag underground pipes or cable before you dig.

Projects in this section include:
- Simple Gravel Pathway
- Pebbled Stepping Stone Path
- Timber & Gravel Garden Steps
- Flagstone Garden Steps
- Zen Garden
- Foundation Drainage Garden
- Sandset Flagstone Patio
- Mortared Flagstone Patio
- Cobblestone Paver Patio
- Stone Fire Pit
- Stone Retaining Wall
- Interlocking Block Retaining Wall
- Stone Garden Wall
- Arroyo
- Freeform Meditation Pond

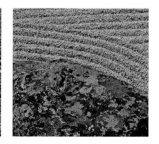

Simple Gravel Pathway

Loose-fill gravel pathways are perfect for stone gardens, casual yards, and other situations where a hard surface is not required. The material is inexpensive, and its fluidity accommodates curves and irregular edging. Since gravel may be made from any rock, gravel paths may be matched to larger stones in the environment, tying them to the earth. The "gravel" need not be restricted to stone, either. Industrial and agricultural by-products like cinders & ashes, walnut shells, seashells, and ceramic fragments may be used as path material.

For a more stable path, choose angular over rounded materials. If you expect to spend time meandering along your new pathway in a shoeless state, however, your feet will be better served with smoother stones such as river rock or pond pebbles. When stone is used, look for a crushed product in the ¼ inch (.6 cm) to ¾ inch (1.9 cm) range. Angular or smooth, stones smaller than that can be tracked into the house, while larger materials are uncomfortable and potentially hazardous to walk on. Use light-colored gravel such as buff limestone to create pathways. Visually, it is much easier to follow a light pathway at night because it reflects more moonlight.

Stable edging helps keep the pathway gravel from migrating into the surrounding mulch and soil. When integrated with landscape fabric, the edge keeps invasive perennials and trees from sending roots and shoots into the path. Do not use gravel paths near plants and trees that produce messy fruits, seeds, or other debris that will be difficult to remove from the gravel. Organic matter left on gravel paths will eventually rot into compost that will support weed seedlings.

A paver-base bed (compactable gravel) under the surface gravel keeps the pathway firm underfoot. For best results, embed the surface gravel material into the paver base by vibrating it with a plate compactor. This prevents the base from showing through if the gravel at the surface is disturbed. An underlayment of landscape fabric helps stabilize the pathway and blocks weeds, but if you don't mind pulling an occasional dandelion and are building on firm soil it can be omitted.

TOOLS & MATERIALS

- 1 × 3 stakes
- 1 × 2 lumber
- Straight 2 × 4
- Mason's string
- Mallet
- Hose or rope
- Landscaping paint
- Measuring tape
- Plate compactor (rental) or hand tamper
- Edging
- Spun bonded landscape fabric
- Sod stripper
- Compactable gravel
- Dressed gravel for surface
- Wheelbarrow
- Round-nosed spade
- Edging/trenching spade
- Flat-nosed spade

Gravel Pathway

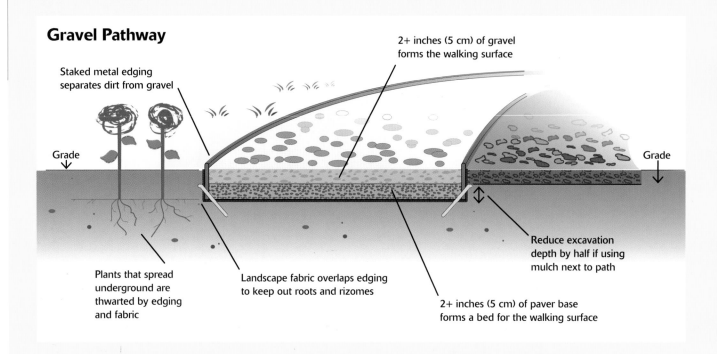

Staked metal edging separates dirt from gravel

2+ inches (5 cm) of gravel forms the walking surface

Grade

Grade

Plants that spread underground are thwarted by edging and fabric

Landscape fabric overlaps edging to keep out roots and rizomes

Reduce excavation depth by half if using mulch next to path

2+ inches (5 cm) of paver base forms a bed for the walking surface

Make a spacer gauge

To ensure that the edges of the pathway are exactly parallel, create a spacer bar and use it as a guide to install the edging. Start with a piece of 2 × 4 that's a bit longer than the path width. Near one end, cut a notch that will fit snugly over the edging. Trim the spacer so the distance from the notch to the other end is the planned width of the pathway.

How to Make a Gravel Pathway

1. Lay out one edge of the path excavation. Use a section of hose or rope to create curves and use stakes and string to indicate straight sections. Cut a supply of 1×2 spacers to set the path width (3½ ft. [107 cm] as seen here) so you can establish the second pathway edge. Use a second hose or rope for curves and stakes and string for straight sections. Mark both edges in landscape paint.

2. Remove soil to a depth of 4" (10 cm) to 6" (15 cm). Use a sod stripper to remove sod and a mattock to remove larger plants and weeds from the path of your excavation. Measure down from a 2×4 placed across the path bed to fine tune this excavation. Grade the bottom of the excavation flat using a garden rake. Note that if mulch will be used outside the path, the excavation should be shallower by the depth of the mulch. Compact the soil with a power plate compactor.

3. Lay landscaping fabric from edge to edge, lapping over the undisturbed ground on either side of the path. On curved paths, it's easier to lay the fabric across the path and overlap the seams by 6" (15 cm).

1 Lay out the outlines of the pathway using a garden hose, spacers and string and stakes. Mark the final outline on the ground with landscape paint.

2 Remove the turf and soil in the layout area. If the grass is in good shape, use a sod stripper to cut away the turf so you can reuse it elsewhere in your yard. Compact the area with a plate compactor.

3 Buy quality landscape fabric that's about 6" (15 cm) wider than the pathway and lay it out directly on the excavated ground. Seams should overlap by 6" (15 cm) or more.

4. Install edging over the fabric. Shim it with small stones so the top edge is ½" (13 mm) above grade (if the path passes through grass) or 2" (5 cm) above grade (if it passes through a mulched landscape). Pound in the edging spikes. To position and spike the second edge, use a 2 × 4 spacer bar that's been notched to fit over your edging (see page 82).

5. Optional: Stone or vertical-brick edges may be set in deeper trenches at the sides of the path. Place these on top of the fabric also. You do not have to use additional edging with paver edging, but the metal edging will keep the pavers from wandering.

6. Completely install the edging material on both edges of the pathway, making sure the edging is a constant distance above grade throughout. Visually inspect the edging to see if the two edges run parallel. Trim off excess fabric so it is level with the tops of the edging. Fill in behind the edging with dirt and tamp down carefully with the end of a 2 x 4 to stiffen the edging.

7. Place a 2"- to 4" (5 to 10 cm)-thick layer of compactable paver base in the excavation and rake it out flat. Lay a thin layer of your surface gravel over the paver base.

4 Drive spikes through the holes in the edging material to pin it to the ground. Be sure to install the edging over the landscape fabric.

5 Brick pavers installed on-end (called soldier style) make an effective edging that has a more formal appearance.

6 After the edging is installed, pack some dirt into the voids behind it to help keep it from slumping or shifting when the fill material is installed.

7 Pour a 2"-thick (5 cm) layer of compactable gravel into the excavation area and rake it smooth. On top of the compactable gravel add a thin layer of the surface gravel you'll be dressing the walkway with.

8. Tamp the compactable gravel and thin layer of surface gravel with a plate compactor. Use care here to avoid contacting, disturbing or breaking the edging. A power tamper or plate compactor can be rented at local hardware, landscaping, or home-improvement centers. This rental is typically daily, so plan ahead.

9. Pour in the remaining surface gravel. Grade the loose gravel so it is level with the edging by dragging a 2 x 4 across the edging tops.

10. Using the plate compactor (or a hand tamper, if you prefer, compact the top layer of gravel. Tamping this layer will help keep the gravel from migrating out of the walk, especially if you are using angular gravel such as trap rock.

11. Finally, rinse off the new walkway with a hose to wash off dirt and dust. You'll be amazed what a difference clean gravel makes in the color and appearance.

8 Spread a thin layer of surface gravel over the compactable gravel and tamp the two layers together with a plate compactor.

9 Fill the pathway area with gravel and then drag a 2 x 4 across the tops of the edging in a sawing motion to level the gravel.

10 Tamp the top layer of gravel so the surface is slightly below the edging.

11 Rinse off the dust from the pathway surface with a hose.

Pebbled Stepping Stone Path

Laying stepping stones creates a practical and appealing way to traverse a garden. With stepping stones providing foot landings, you are free to put pretty much any type of infill between the stones. Gravel, smooth stones, ceramic toads—if you don't have to walk on it, anything goes. Some people place stepping stones on individual footings over ponds and streams, making water the temporary infill that surrounds the stones. The infill does not need to follow a narrow path bed, either. Steppers can be used to cross a broad expanse of gravel, such as a Zen gravel panel, or a smaller graveled opening in an alpine rock garden.

Stepping stones in a path do two jobs: they lead the eye and they carry the traveler. In both cases the goal is rarely fast direct transport, but more of a relaxing meander that's comfortable, slow-paced, and above all natural. Arrange the stepping stones in a walking path according to the gaits and strides of the people most likely to use the pathway. Realize that our gaits tend to be longer on a utility path than in a rock garden.

Sometimes steppers are placed more for visual effect, with the knowledge that they will break the pacing rule with artful clusters of stones. Clustering is also an effective way to slow or congregate walkers near a Y in the path or at a good vantage point for a striking feature of the garden.

Choose steppers and pebbles that are complementary in color. Shades of medium to dark gray are a popular combination for a Zen feeling. Too much contrast or very bright colors tend to undermine the sense of tranquility a pebbled stepping stone path can achieve.

In the project featured here, landscape edging is used to contain the loose infill material (small aggregate). A stepping stone path can also be very effective without edging. For example, setting a series of steppers directly into your lawn and letting the lawn grass grow between them.

TOOLS & MATERIALS

- 1 × 3 stakes
- 1 × 2 lumber
- Straight 2 × 4
- Mason's string
- Mallet
- Hose or rope
- Landscaping paint
- Measuring tape
- Edging
- Spun bonded landscape fabric
- Sod stripper
- Coarse sand
- Thick steppers or broad river rocks with one flat face
- ¼" to ½" (6 mm to 12 mm) pond pebbles
- 2½" (6 mm) dia. river rock
- Wheelbarrow
- Round-nosed spade
- Edging/trenching spade
- Flat-nosed spade
- Hand tamper

Choosing Steppers

Select beefy stones (minimum 2½" [6 cm] to 3½" [9 cm] thick) with at least one flat side. Thinner stepping stones tend to sink into the pebble infill. Stones that are described as stepping stones usually have two flat faces. For the visual effect we sought on this project, we chose steppers and 12 to 24" wide fieldstones with one broad, flat face (the rounded face is buried in the ground, naturally).

Fieldstone with a flat face

Steppers

How to Make a Pebbled Stepping Stone Path

1. Excavate and prepare a bed for the path as you would for the gravel pathway (pages 82 to 84), but use coarse building sand instead of compactable paver-base. Screed the sand flat 2" (5 cm) below the top of the edging. Do not tamp the sand. You may use any edging material you like. Low-profile plastic landscape edging is a good choice because it does not compete with the pathway.

2. Position the stepping stones in the coarse sand bedding, spacing them based on the average slow-walk stride of the people who will use the path. Orient the stones to create a pleasing composition. Staggering them in a left/right fashion is a common practice. Strive for a layout that's both comfortable to walk and attractive to look at. They can be in a fairly regular, left/right pattern or arranged into clusters for a more interesting appearance. Add or remove sand beneath the steppers until they are stable and even with one another.

1 Excavate the pathway site and prepare a foundation as shown in the Gravel Pathway project (pages 82 to 84). Substitute coarse building sand for compactable gravel. Strike the sand to a consistent depth with a notched 2 × 4.

2 Level the stones by adding and removing sand until they are solidly seated. On flat runs, you should be able to rest a flat 2 × 4 on three stones at once, making solid contact with each. It is much easier to pack sand under stones if you moisten the sand first. Also moisten the sand bed to prevent sand from drifting.

Move from a formal area to a less orderly area of your yard by creating a pathway that begins with closely spaced steppers on the formal end and gradually transforms into a mostly-gravel path on the casual end, with only occasional clusters of steppers.

3. Pour in a layer of the larger infill stones (2" dia. river rock is seen here). Smooth the stones with a garden rake. They should be below the tops of the stepping stones. Reserve about one-third of the larger diameter rocks.

4. Add the smaller diameter infill, which will migrate down and fill in around the larger infill rocks. To help settle the rocks you can tamp lightly with a hand tamper, but don't get too aggressive—the larger rocks will fracture fairly easily.

5. Scatter the remaining larger diameter infill stones across the infill area so they float on top of the other stones. Eventually, they will sink down lower in the pathway and you will need to lift and replace them selectively to maintain the original appearance.

3 If you're using two or more sizes of infill, start by spreading out a layer of the largest diameter rock.

4 Add the smallest size infill stones last, spreading them evenly so you do not have to rake them much.

5 Place the remaining larger-diameter infill stones around the surface of the walkway to enhance the visual effect of the pathway.

Timber & Gravel Garden Steps

Timber framed steps provide a delightfully simple and structurally satisfying way of managing slopes. They are usually designed with shallow steps that have long runs and large tread areas, which can be filled with materials found elsewhere in your landscape. In the project featured here we use gravel (small aggregate river rock), a common surface for paths and rock gardens. Other tread surfaces include bricks, cobbles and stepping stones. Even large flagstones can be sawn and snapped to fit the tread openings.

Timber steps needn't follow the straight and narrow, either. You can vary the lengths of the left and right returns to create swooping helical steps that suggest spiral staircases. Or, increase the length of both returns to create a broad landing on which to set pots or accommodate a natural flattening of the slope. Want to soften the steps? Use soil as a base near the sides of the steps and plant herbs or groundcovers. Or for a spring surprise, plant daffodils under a light pea gravel top dressing at the edges of the steps.

Timber steps don't require deep footings, as the wooden joints flex with the earth rather than crack like concrete. We do recommend some underground anchoring, however, to keep loose muddy soil from pushing the steps forward. To provide this, the steps shown here attach to a timber cleat at the base of the slope. As with any steps, keep step size consistent so people don't trip.

Designing steps is an important part of the process. Determine the total rise and run of the hill and translate this into a step size that conforms to the formula 2x (rise) + run = 26 inches (66 cm). Your step rise will equal your timber width, which will be 3½ inches (9 cm) (4 × 4 or 4 × 6 on the flat), 5½ inch (14 cm) (6 × 6 or 4 × 6 on edge) or 7½ inches (19 cm) (8 × 8). See pages 24 to 25 for more information on designing steps.

TOOLS & MATERIALS

- Wood stakes
- Mason's string
- String level
- Straight 2 × 4
- Level
- Measuring tape
- Excavating tools
- Hand tamper
- Compactable gravel
- Sand
- Gravel
- Landscape timbers
- Circular saw
- Speed square
- Framing square
- ⅜" (1 cm) landscape spikes up to 12" (30 cm) long depending on timbers
- Drill and ⅜" (1cm) dia. bit with long shaft
- Sledge hammer

Gravel & Timber Garden Steps

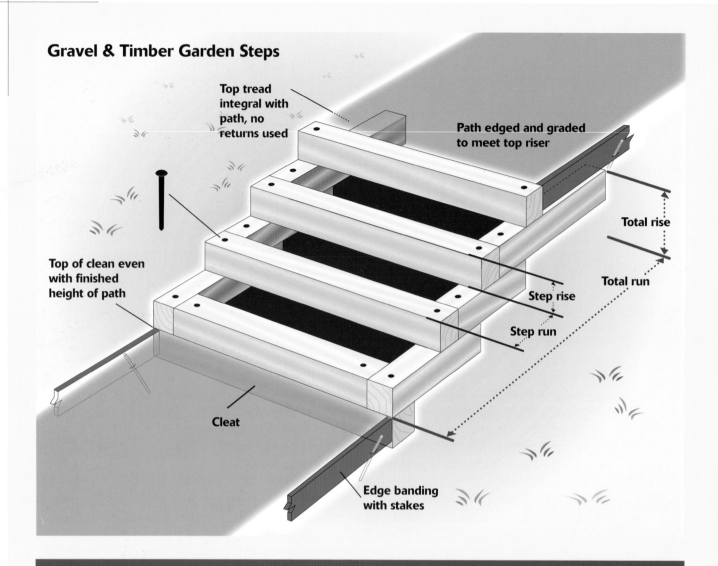

Top tread integral with path, no returns used

Path edged and graded to meet top riser

Total rise

Step rise

Total run

Step run

Top of clean even with finished height of path

Cleat

Edge banding with stakes

Cutting Timbers

Large landscape timbers (6 x 6" and bigger) can be cut accurately and squarely with a circular saw, even though the saw's cutting capacity isn't big enough to do the job in one pass. First, draw cutting lines on all four sides of the timber using a speed square as guide. Next, cut along the line on all four sides with the saw set for maximum blade depth. Finally, use a hand saw to finish the cut. For most DIYers, this will yield a straighter cut than saws that can make the cut in one pass, such as a reciprocating saw.

Timber & Gravel Garden Steps

1. Mark the starting and end points and the side outlines for the project on the ground using landscape paint. Timber width determines the step rise (the height) as well as the recommended run (depth) of each step (see pages 24 to 25). The steps are anchored by a landscape timber buried at the foot of the steps, called the cleat. Dig a trench for the cleat at the base of the stairs, gauging the depth so the top of the cleat is level with the top of the pathway leading up to the steps (if there is one), factoring in a 2" to 4" (5 cm to 10 cm) layer of compactable gravel. Compact some gravel into the trench to level the base for positioning the cleat. Cut the cleat to length, set it into the trench and level it by packing in and removing gravel.

2. The timbers that run back into the hill, perpendicular to the cleat and risers, are called returns. They should be long enough to anchor the riser and returns from the step above (tread width plus the thickness of the next riser plus about a 6" (15 cm) to support the second returns). Dig trenches back into the hill for the returns and compact gravel into the trenches so each return sits level on the cleat and gravel.

3. Cut and position the returns and the first riser. Using a 2 × 4 as a level extender, check to see if the backs of the returns are level with each other and adjust by adding or removing gravel. Drill four ³/₈" (1 cm) holes and attach the first riser and the two returns to the cleat with spikes.

1 Bury a timber at the foot of the first step to serve as a cleat for anchoring the steps. The top should be level and flush with the top of the pathway.

2 Prepare the site for the returns by tamping some compactable gravel into each trench.

3 Drill a ³/₈" (1 cm) pilot hole at each joint between the riser and the returns and the cleat. Drive ³/₈" (1 cm) spikes into each hole to fasten the members together.

4 Check the second set of returns for level and then attach them to the returns below with spikes driven into pilot holes..

4. Excavate and pack in gravel for the second set of returns. Cut and position the second riser across the front ends of the first returns, leaving the correct unit run between the riser faces. Note that only the first riser doesn't span the full width of the steps. Cut and position the returns, check for level and then pre-drill and spike the risers and returns as indicated.

5. Construct the remaining steps in the same fashion. As you build, it may be necessary to alter the grade of the slope with additional excavating or backfilling (few naturally occurring hills form with a perfectly even slope). Grade the earth so a fairly regular reveal of the side returns is shown and the earth surrounding the steps is never higher than the nearby treads.

6. Finish installing the timbers. At the top, you may leave the returns off because this tread should be integral with the path. The top of the last riser should be slightly higher than the surrounding ground. Returns may be used to contain the pathway material at the top of the steps if you wish.

5 Backfill or excavate around the sides of the steps as needed.

6 Install the top timber (no returns) by attaching it to the returns below with spikes.

7. Lay a base of compactable gravel in each stair tread area. Tamp the material with the butt of a 2 × 4 or a 4 × 4 to compact it. Avoid tamping layers that are too thick—limit each layer to 2", tamp it, and then add another layer.

8. Fill up the tread areas with gravel or any other decorative dressing materials you choose. For maximum stability, choose an irregular crushed gravel over smooth, rounded stones. The irregular surfaces knit together a little more effectively. Smooth stones, like the river rock seen here, blend into the environment more naturally and feel better under foot.

9. Create or improve pathways at the top and bottom of the steps. For nice effect, build a loose fill walkway using the same type of gravel that you used for the steps. (See Gravel Pathway, pages 80 to 85).

7 Install a layer of compactable gravel at the bottom of each tread opening. Tamp with the butt end of a 2 × 2 or 4 × 4.

8 Add the gravel layer on top of the compacted base. Fill each tread cavity to the top and replenish with gravel as needed.

9 Finish the pathways that tie into the top and bottom of the stairs. Add a railing if desired or if required by your local building codes.

Flagstone Garden Steps

Flagstone steps are perfect structures for managing low slopes. They consist of broad flagstone treads and blocky ashlar risers, commonly sold as wall stone. The risers are prepared with compactable gravel beds on which the flagstone treads rest. For the project featured here, we purchased both the flagstone and the wall stone in their natural split state (as opposed to sawn). It may seem like overkill, but you should plan on purchasing 40 percent more flagstone, by square foot coverage, than your plans say you need. The process of fitting the stones together involves a lot of cutting and waste.

The average height of your risers is defined by the height of the wall stone available to you. These rough stones are separated and sold in a range of thicknesses (such as 3 inch to 4 inch [8 cm to 10 cm]), but hand picking the stones helps bring them into a tighter range. The more uniform the thicknesses of your blocks, the less shimming and adjusting you'll have to do.

Flagstone steps work best when you create the broadest possible treads: think of them as a series of terraced patios. The goal, once you have you stock in hand, is to create tread surface with as few stones as possible. This generally means you'll be doing quite a bit of cutting to get the irregular shapes that are the hallmark of flagstone to fit together. For more formal looking results, you can cut the flagstones along straight lines so they fit together with small, regular gaps. Some designers prefer this look, while other feel it eliminates the natural charm to which flagstone owes much of its popularity. Sawn flag patios often are mortared to a concrete slab base and have solid mortar in the gaps.

Before you start building your steps, be sure to read the section on determining the ideal step rise and run (pages 24 to 25). You will also need to stock up on slivers of rocks to use as shims to bring your risers and returns to a consistent height. Breaking and cutting your stone generally produces plenty of these.

TOOLS & MATERIALS

- Stakes
- Mason's string
- Landscape marking paint
- String level
- Straight 2 × 4
- Torpedo level
- 4-ft. level
- Measuring tape
- Excavating tools
- Spun bonded landscape fabric
- Compactable gravel
- Coarse sand
- 3-pound (1.4 kg) maul
- Hand tamper
- Wall stone
- Flagstones
- Stone and block adhesive

Flagstone Garden Steps

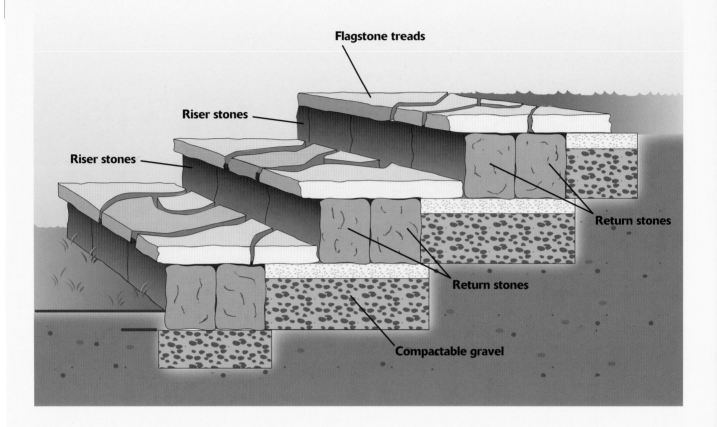

Flagstone treads

Riser stones

Riser stones

Return stones

Return stones

Compactable gravel

Steps from Cast Blocks & Pavers

Manmade pavers and concrete blocks can be used to create landscape steps. Typical cast products will result in steps that have a much more regular, formal appearance than relatively freeform flagstones. But the uniform sizes and shapes greatly simplify the job of making your steps even and comfortable to walk upon. The concrete blocks in the steps seen here are precast, rectangular step forms that are designed to hold loose fill or pavers when they are stacked together. Cast step forms are difficult to locate, but you can accomplish a similar effect by building and stacking wood forms of the same dimension using treated lumber or by casting your own concrete step forms.

How to Make Flagstone Garden Steps

1. Determine the rise and run of the slope and calculate the rise, run, and number of steps needed (see pages 24 to 25). Plot the footprint of your steps on the ground in landscaping paint. Purchase wall stones for your risers and returns in a height equal to the unit rise of your steps. Buy up to 40 percent more flagstone than needed to cover the treads.

2. Excavate for the first step to a depth that will provide at least 4" of compactable gravel and an inch of sand beneath the first flagstone tread. Dig deeper to create a trench under the first risers and returns, so that these may have at least 4" of compactable base underneath. The first riser is sunk into the ground to a depth equal to the average thickness of the flagstone. Use wall stone returns only near risers to fill gaps where the risers project out of the ground.

3. Compact the soil in the wall-stone trench using the butt of a 2 × 4 or 4 × 4 post. Layer in compactable gravel to within an inch of the planned height and tamp. Lay in a top layer of compactable gravel and level it side-to-side and back-to-front. This top layer of gravel should be a flagstone's thickness below grade. This will keep the rise of the first step the same as the following steps. Do not compact the second layer of gravel—risers should be set on looser gravel so their height may be adjusted more readily.

1 Thread a line level onto a mason's string and tie the ends of the string to stakes at the top and bottom of the stair installation site. With the string level, measure the difference in distance from the string to the ground at the top and bottom of the steps to find the total run. See pages 24 to 25 for more help on designing steps.

2 Excavate for the first step and the stone walls risers and returns. Dig deep enough to accommodate 4" of compactable gravel and 1" of sand throughout. This means you'll be excavating a shallow area for the tread and a deeper U-shaped trench for the wall stones.

3 Pour a layer of compactable gravel into the U-shaped trench for the wall stones. Compact the gravel with a tamper or post and then top it off with another layer that should not be compacted.

4. Set the riser stones and one or two return stones onto the gravel base. Level the riser stones side to side by laying a level across the stones and adding or removing gravel as needed. Level the risers front to back with a torpedo level. Allow for a slight up slope for the returns. Seat the stones firmly in the gravel with a hand maul, but protect the stone with a wood block.

5. Line the area you excavated for the first tread with landscape fabric, draping it up to cover the insides of the risers and returns. Add layers of compactable gravel and tamp down to within an inch of the tops of the risers and returns. Fill the remainder of the bed with sand and level it side-to-side with a section of 2 x 4. Slope it slightly from the back down to the front so the treads will drain. This layer of sand should be a little above your risers and returns so that the tread stones will compact down to sit on the wall stones.

6. Measure the step/run distance back from the face of your first risers and set a masons line across the sand bed. Set the second set of risers and returns as you did the first, except the risers don't need to be dug in on the bottom because the bottom tread will reduce the risers' effective height.

4 Position the riser stones and the return stones in the trench and level them. Add or remove gravel as necessary and then rap them gently on the tops with a hand maul to set them. Use a wood block to protect the stones from the maul.

5 Line the area under the first tread with landscape fabric. Cover it with a layer of compactable gravel and then a layer of sand.

6 Lay the second course of risers, using a level mason's string as a reference.

7. Fold fabric over the tops of the risers and trim off the excess. Now, set the flagstone treads of the first step like a puzzle, leaving a consistent distance between stones. Use large, heavy stones with relatively straight edges at the front of the step, overhanging the risers by about 2" (5 cm). It is useful to sort your stone stock before you start laying flags so you can identify the best candidates for the featured positions at the front of the step.

8. Fill in with smaller stones near the back. Cut and dress stones where necessary (see pages 56 to 61). Finding a good arrangement takes some trial-and-error. Try to maintain somewhat regular gaps and avoid having stones that are too small. Ideally, all stones should be at least as large as a dinner plate.

9. Using a level as a guide, adjust the stones so the treads form a flat surface. Add sand under thinner stones and remove sand from beneath thicker stones until all the flags come close to touching the level and are stable.

7 Begin laying out the flagstone treads. It's best to use large stones with straight front edges at the fronts of the steps.

8 Fill in gaps between larger stones by trimming smaller pieces to fit. Shoot for consistent gaps. Don't let the stones touch one another when placed.

9 Pack wet sand underneath low areas and remove sand underneath high areas until all the flags on the tread are basically flat and even.

10. Do not use sand to shim the wall stones. Instead, adhere thin shards of stone to the wall stone risers with block and stone adhesive. Make sure there is no path for sand to wash out from beneath the treads. You may settle smaller stones in sand with a mallet, but cushion your blows with a short length of wood.

11. Build the next step in the same manner as the first. On this one, however, you do not need to make a U-shaped trench for the risers—the bottoms of the risers should be at the same height as the bottoms of the tread on the step below. However, you may need to excavate for the return stones so the stones in each return will be level to one another. The top step often will not require returns.

12. Dump coarse, dark sand such as granite sand over the stones and sweep it into the joints to fill them. Or, choose polymeric sand, which resists wash-out better than regular builders sand. Inspect the steps regularly for the first few weeks and make adjustments to height of stones as needed.

10 Use thin pieces of broken stone as shims to raise wall stones to their required level. Make sure the stone shims are sturdy enough that they won't flake apart easily. Use block and stone adhesive to hold the shims in place.

11 Continue adding steps and making your way up the slope. You shouldn't need to trench for the risers, but you may need to move some dirt so you can pack it in and install the return stones.

12 Fill the joints between stones with coarse sand to bind them together and for a more finished appearance.

Stone Step Variations

Timbers & brick pavers contribute interesting texture and pattern to a landscape. Construction is similar to the timber and concrete project shown on the preceding pages.

Flagstone steps create a rustic pathway in a natural garden setting. They can be installed using the natural hill slope as a riser.

Mortared brick steps are ideal in homes and landscapes with a classic or traditional style.

Concrete and natural stone create an elegant and uniform walkway for a gentle slope.

Zen Garden

What's commonly called a "Zen Garden" in the West is actually a Japanese dry garden, with little historical connection to Zen Buddhism. The form typically consists of sparse, carefully positioned stones in a meticulously raked bed of coarse sand or fine gravel. Japanese dry gardens can be immensely satisfying. Proponents find the uncluttered space calming and the act of raking out water-like ripples in the gravel soothing and perhaps even healing. The fact that they are low-maintenance and drought resistant is another advantage.

Site your garden on flat or barely-sloped ground away from messy trees and shrubs (and cats), as gravel and sand are eventually spoiled by the accumulation of organic matter. There are many materials you can use as the rakable medium for the garden. Generally, lighter colored, very coarse sand is preferred—it needs to be small enough to be raked into rills yet large enough that the rake lines don't settle out immediately. Crushed granite is a viable medium. Another option that is used occasionally is turkey grit, a fine gravel available from farm supply outlets. In this project, we show you how to edge your garden with cast pavers set on edge, although you may prefer to use natural stone blocks or even smooth stones in the 4 to 6 inches (10 to 15 cm) range.

Most Zen gardens feature a few specimen rocks, including some larger smooth stones that add new textures and tall, angular stones that are set on-end and symbolize trees. You can place one specimen in the center of the garden to feature it, or place several smaller stones around the area in groupings or cairns. On larger gardens it makes some design sense to install a flat stone or two so you can use them like stepping stones and navigate the garden without disturbing the raking medium.

If you will be leaving your Zen rock garden unattended for a period of time, cover it with a weighted tarp to prevent the accumulation of debris (unless you find picking leaves out of gravel to be relaxing too).

TOOLS & MATERIALS

- Stakes
- Mason's string
- Garden hose
- Landscape marking paint
- Straight 2 × 4
- Level

- Measuring tape
- Excavating tools
- Compactable gravel
- Crushed granite (light colored)
- Hand maul
- Manual tamper

- Spun bonded landscape fabric
- Field stone steppers
- Specimen stones
- Border stones or blocks

How to Make a Zen Garden

1. Mark out the area of your garden with hoses or ropes for smooth curves and with mason's string between stakes for straight lines. When you are satisfied with the dimensions, trace your layout lines onto the ground with landscape marking paint. If possible, site the garden so it is not directly under any "dirty" trees that shed leaves and debris.

2. Clear any weeds or sod from the area and excavate the entire project area to a depth of around 3" (8 cm). Install any large stones specimen stones or other features (such as a landscape bridge) that require further excavation.

3. Dig a 6 to 8" (15 to 20 cm) deep trench for the border stones or pavers you'll be installing around the garden perimeter. Compact the soil in the trench with a hand tamper, or the butt of a 4 × 4 post.

4. Fill perimeter trench with 3" (8 cm) of compactable gravel and tamp. Add a loose inch of compactable gravel on top of the trench area and smooth out with a garden rake. Lay landscape fabric over the work area, overlapping seams and cutting out for specimen stones.

5. Set cast pavers or natural stone blocks into the gravel-filled trench with their edges touching. Place a long straight 2 × 4 over the blocks to check for flatness. Pound down high blocks with a

Setting Specimen Stones

Bury at least one-third of a tall boulder or ledge stone for stability. Even squat boulders should be buried below the point at which they slope back toward the center. This way, they look like a natural part of the landscape.

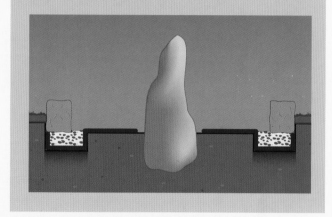

mallet, protecting the blocks with a scrap of 2 × 4. Level the blocks front to back with a torpedo level.

1 Lay out the garden location using stakes and string or hoses and then mark the outline directly onto the ground with landscape paint.

2 Excavate the site and install any large specimen stones that require burial more than a half foot below grade.

3 Dig a trench around the border for the border stones.

4 Pour a 3" (8 cm) thick layer of compactable gravel into the border trench and tamp down with a post or a hand tamper.

5 Place border blocks into the trench and adjust them so the tops are even.

6. Trim off excess landscape fabric and backfill to both sides of this edge with gravel or sand. Experiment with the positioning of stepping stones, island stones, and other smaller stones in the garden until you arrive at a pleasing composition that provides adequate footing from which to rake the gravel.

7. Once you've devised an arrangement you like, set the stones onto individual beds of sand about an inch deep. Adjust the height of the stepping or island stones by adding or removing sand so they will "float" comfortably above the gravel, when it's laid.

8. Fill the garden area with a 2" to 4" (5 cm to 10 cm) layer of your raking medium—crushed granite is shown here. Dampen it slightly before raking to form ripples in your dry "sea." Maintenance of the garden is, of course, the point. Re-rake to relax.

6 Test different configurations of rocks in the garden to find an arrangement you like. If it's a larger garden, strategically place a few flat rocks so you can reach the entire garden with a rake without stepping in the raking medium.

7 Set the stones in position on individual beds of sand about 1" (3 cm) thick.

8 Rake the medium into pleasing patterns with a special rake (see next page).

How to Make a Zen Garden Rake

Once you have constructed your Zen garden, you will use two tools to interact with it: your eyes and a good rake. While any garden rake will suffice for creating the swirling and concentric rills that are hallmarks of the Zen garden, a special rake that's dedicated to the garden will enhance your hands-on interaction.

Many Zen garden rakes are constructed from bamboo. Bamboo is lightweight and readily available in the East. While you can certainly choose this material, you're likely to find that the lightness can actually work against it, causing you to exert more strain to cut through the raking medium. A rake made from solid wood has greater heft that lets it glide more smoothly through the medium. The rake show here is made using only the following materials:

- 1¼"-dia. by 48" (3.2 cm × 1.2 m) oak or pine dowel (handle)
- ½" by 36" (.3 mm × .9 m) oak or pine dowel (tines)
- 2 x 3 × 9½" (5 cm × 8 cm x 24 cm) piece of red oak (head)

Figure 1

Figure 2

Figure 3

Here is how to make it. Start by sanding all of the stock very smooth using sandpaper up to150 grit in coarseness. Soften the edges of the 2 × 3 with the sandpaper. Drill a 1¼" (3.2 cm) dia. hole in the head for the handle (figure 1). The hole should go all the way through the head at a 22½° downward angle (half of a 45° angle), with the top of the hole no closer than ¾" (2 cm) to the top of the head. Use a backer board when drilling to prevent blowout and splinters.

Next, drill ½" (13 mm) dia. by 1" (3 cm) deep seat holes for the tines in the bottom edge of the blank. Locate centers of the two end holes 1" (3 cm) from the ends. Measure in 2½" (6 cm) from each end hole and mark centers for the intermediate tines. Use masking tape to mark a drilling depth of 1" (3 cm) on your drill bit and then drill perpendicular holes at each

centerline. Cut four 5" (13 cm) long pieces of the ½" (13 mm) dia. oak doweling for the tines. Apply wood glue into the bottom of each hole and insert the tines, setting them by gently tapping with a wood mallet (figure 2). Then, apply glue to the handle holes sides and insert the handle so the end protrudes all the way through. After the glue dries, drill a ½" (13 mm) dia. hole down through the top of the head and into the handle. Glue a ½" (13 mm) dowel into the hole to reinforce the handle (this is called pinning).

Finally, use a back saw, gentleman's saw or Japanese flush-cutting saw to trim the handle end and the handle pin flush with the head (figure 3). Sand to smooth the trimmed ends and remove any dried glue. Finish with two or three light coats of wipe-on polyurethane tinted for red oak.

Foundation Drainage Garden

Does your home suffer from a basement that's perpetually wet? Sloping your landscaping and hard surfaces away from the house may be enough to correct the problem. Sometimes, however, the erosion protection of a soil covering is desired. If that's the case, a foundation drainage garden may be for you. The dual function of the garden is to enhance your landscape and keep your basement dry by directing runoff water safely away from the foundation.

The first objective with foundation drainage is to prevent water from puddling near your house. You want it to exit the area quickly and efficiently. Check the slope near your foundation walls with a level that's set on top of a long straight 2 x 4 to see if the water can naturally run away from your house. Runoff from houses often flows to a swale—a long, sloping depression about 10 ft. from the house and parallel to the wall.

When the regrading is done and sufficient slope has been established, you can install a drainage garden. Consisting of a waterproof underlayment covered with soil or rocks (or some combination of the two), drainage gardens have the added bonus of being virtually maintenance free. It is recommended, however, that you add plant cover for visual appeal.

If raising the grade next to a foundation wall causes the new ground-level to be within 2 inch (5 cm) of a basement window, you'll need to install a window well to protect the window frame and keep runoff from getting inside through the window.

When selecting a material for top-dressing the drainage garden, be sure to consider visual impac. Look for colors and textures that are native to your area already exist in your yard. Don't choose lava rock unless you live in the shadow of Mount Krakatoa. Mulch, bark and other organic materials do not work as dressing for foundation gardens. They will simply wash away. Similarly, very small aggregate and gravel have a way of disappearing. Crushed aggregate, river rock or field stone in the 2 inch (5 cm) average diameter range is an excellent choice.

TOOLS & MATERIALS

- Stakes
- Mason's string
- Chalk line
- Grease pencil
- Hose
- Landscape marking paint

- Straight 2 × 4
- Level
- Folding rule
- Excavating tools
- Rototiller
- Garden rake
- Spun bonded landscape fabric

- Lawn edging
- Edging spikes
- Hand maul
- Lawn roller
- Gravel
- Utility knife

Foundation Drainage Garden

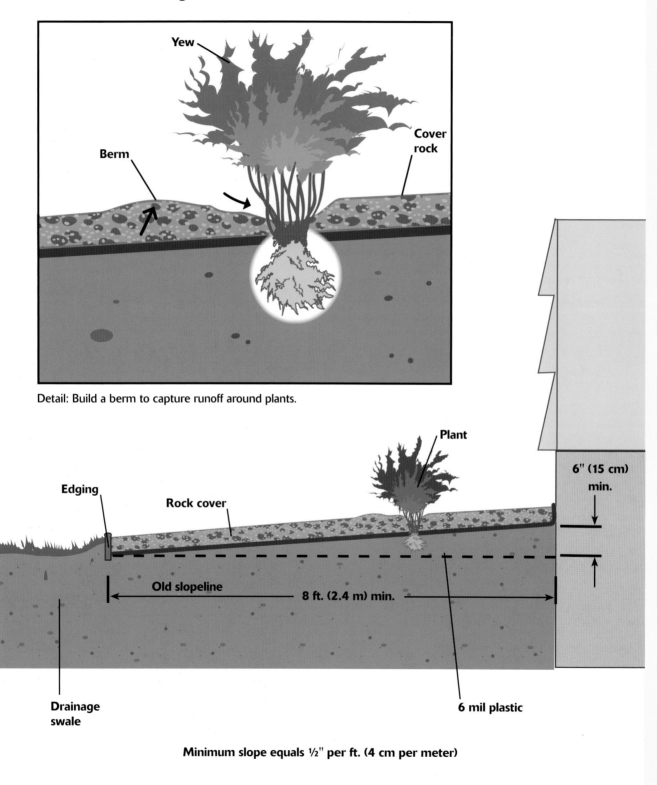

Detail: Build a berm to capture runoff around plants.

Minimum slope equals ½" per ft. (4 cm per meter)

A DRAINAGE GARDEN **slopes away from your house to direct water runoff away from the foundation.**

How to Make a Foundation Drainage Garden

1. Clear all plantings, landscape rock, landscape fabric and other debris from the construction site. Using an 8-ft. (2.4 m)-long 2 × 4 with a level on top, mark where the grade needs to fall at the house in order to produce about a minimum 6" (15 cm) drop from the house to a point 8 ft. (2.4 m) away. Repeat the procedure every 10 ft. (3 m) along the foundation wall. Connect the grade points with snapped chalk lines.

2. Lay out the outer edge of the garden. Use a hose or rope to lay out curves and draw a mason's string between stakes for straight lines. Draw the line on the ground in landscape marking paint. Dig an edge 4" (10 cm) straight down along this line, tossing the soil toward the house.

3. Break up the garden soil, especially near the edge, with a mattock or shovel, and rototill into a smooth, workable medium. Now grade the soil with a garden rake into a flat slope between the bottom of your edge excavation and the grade line on the house.

1 Mark several reference points on your foundation wall to indicate where the top of the new garden needs to begin to be high enough that it can drop off at least 6" (15 cm) at a point 8 ft. (2.4 m) away from the house.

2 Dig out a trench along the lower edge of the garden area, tossing the soil back toward the high end of the garden to begin the regrading work.

3 Smooth out and level off the soil in the work area by first loosening it with a mattock or rototiller and then redistributing and smoothing with a garden rake.

4. Roll the soil in the work area with a water-weighted lawn roller to compact it. Or, if you're up for a workout, use a hand tamper. Add additional soil or sand (if you won't be planting) if the excavation area is more than 4" (10 cm) deep at any point.

5. Position your professional-grade plastic lawn edging in the trench at the base of the garden. The rim tube should be half below grade and the fold at the bottom of the edge should face toward the house. Spike the edge in place using at least one landscape spike per 4 ft. of edging.

6. Cut strips of 6 mil black plastic sheeting to fit in two layers over the garden (the strips should be parallel to the house). If the plastic laps, the pieces nearest the house should be on top. Fold the pieces that butt up against the house so they climb at least 2" (5 cm) up the foundation. Hold plastic in place by spreading shovelfuls of gravel near the corners.

4 Use a lawn roller or a tamper to compact the soil in the garden area. Add new soil to fill in low areas if necessary.

5 Install high-quality plastic edging at the low edge of the garden so the top of the rim tube is slightly above grade.

6 Cover the garden area with strips of 6 mil black plastic sheeting that are laid parallel to the house. Weight the corners with gravel.

7. Plant perennials and shrubs by cutting an X into the plastic, large enough to accommodate the root ball. Fold the plastic flaps under the cutout to create clearance for your shovel as you dig the planting holes. Tip: Put dirt on a square of plywood to keep your plastic clean as you dig. Plant so the top of the root ball will reside near the surface of the gravel. A dip in the grade where the root ball enters the soil will help it accumulate water, which is beneficial to the plant (see page 112).

8. Option: Install drip irrigation hoses with leads near your plantings, if that is needed, and weigh the hoses down with gravel.

9. Fill the area with your selected gravel or landscape rock cover, always dumping the wheelbarrow from the side of the bed or from already-laid gravel. Rake into a 2 to 3" (5 to 8 cm) layer over the plastic. Just barely cover the tops of the root balls with gravel. Tip: Turn your garden rake upside down with the tines up so your rake does not puncture the plastic sheeting.

7 Plant landscape shrubs and other perennials to your taste, taking into account the availability of sunlight. Cut X's in the plastic sheeting to create clearance for the plant root balls. Don't overplant.

8 Option: For convenience of watering, bury drip irrigation lines and leads in the foundation garden.

9 Cover the foundation garden with landscape rock or gravel of your choice. Avoid driving your wheelbarrow over bare plastic.

Sandset Flagstone Patio

Flagstones make a great, long-lasting patio surface, although it may be a little rough and uneven. They are especially suited to curved borders, but the stones may be scored and snapped where they meet buildings. Your landscape will appear more natural if your flagstones are of the same stone species as other stones in your garden. For example, if your gravel paths and walls are made from a local buff limestone, look for the same material in limestone flags.

Flagstones usually come in very large slabs that are sold as "flagstone" or in smaller slabs that are sold as "steppers." You can make a patio out of either. Larger stones will make a more solid patio with a more even surface, but the bigger ones can require three strong people to position, and large stones are hard to cut and fit tightly.

If your soil is well drained and stable, flagstones may be laid on nothing more than a layer of sand. However, if you have unstable clay soils that become soft when wet, lay a deep foundation of compactable gravel (see pages 64 to 65) under your sand.

The spaces between flagstones may be planted with any of a number of low-growing perennials suited to crevice culture. For best results use sand-based soil (see page 12) between flags when planting. For patios that will be planted, stick to very small plants that can withstand foot-traffic. Or transform your "patio" into a flat rock garden, eliminating an occasional small flag in an out of the way spot and planting the space with a sturdy accent species.

TOOLS & MATERIALS

- Sod kicker
- Garden rake
- Hand tamper
- Flat nose spade
- Round nose spade
- Landscape paint
- Mason's line

- Line level
- Stakes
- Long straight 2 × 4s
- 1" (3 cm) dia. outside metal pipes for screed spacers
- Coarse sand

- Flagstones
- Circular saw with diamond blade
- Hand maul
- Cold chisel
- Sand-based soil

Sandset Flagstone Patio

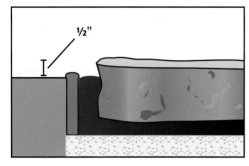

LAY FLAGSTONES so the tops are approximately ½" (13 mm) above ground. Because natural stones are not uniform thickness you will need to adjust sand or dirt beneath each flag individually.

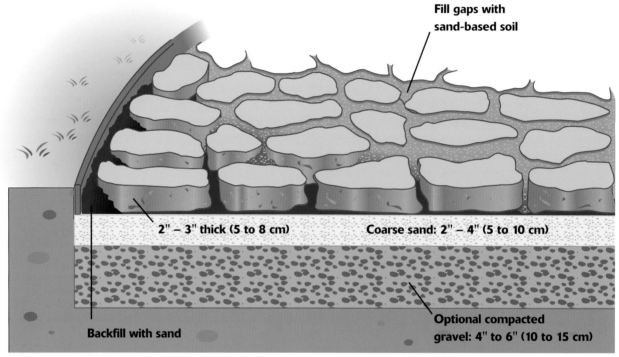

Fill gaps with sand-based soil

2" – 3" thick (5 to 8 cm)   Coarse sand: 2" – 4" (5 to 10 cm)

Backfill with sand

Optional compacted gravel: 4" to 6" (10 to 15 cm)

A TYPICAL SANDSET PATIO OR WALKWAY has a compacted gravel base covered by a layer of coarse sand for embedding the flags. Sand-based soil fills the gaps.

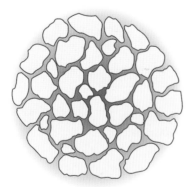

IRREGULAR FLAGSTONES look natural and are easy to work with in round layouts.

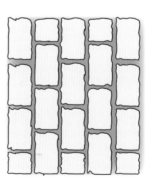

FLAGSTONES THAT ARE CUT into rectangular shapes can be laid in square or rectangular patterns with uniform gaps.

How to Make a Sandset Flagstone Patio

1. Delineate the boundaries of the patio base first using string and stakes for straight lines and a hose or rope for curves. The base should extend 2 to 4" (5 to 10 cm) beyond the edges of the flagstones, except where the patio will butt up to a wall. Trace outlines onto the ground with landscape marking paint once you are satisfied with the layout. (See pages 8 to 19 for more information on designing and siting a patio.)

2. Remove sod and weeds and excavate the base to a flat, slightly pitched plane (see pages 62 to 65). If you need to fill dips, use compactable gravel and compact it with a hand or mechanical tamper. The depth of the base excavation, after gravel and sand are added, should equal the thickness of your flagstones minus ½" (13 mm). This will give the stones a little rise over the surrounding grade when they are sitting on the sand.

3. Lay sections of 1" (3 cm) dia. outside metal pipe across the project area to function as screed gauges. These gauges allow you to strike off sand at a consistent depth when you drag a screed board over them. You can conserve on pipe by screeding smaller sections and then moving the pipe. *Note: Edging is used in most stonescaping projects, but with a sand-set patio the effect can be a bit disharmonious. For best results, create a base that's slightly larger that the patio and allow the neighboring groundcover to grow up to the edges of the patio.*

1 Outline your new patio shape directly onto the ground with landscape paint. Choose a slightly irregular organic shape for a more natural appearance which tends to be effective with sand-set flagstone.

2 Use stakes and strings to establish level lines in the project area. This allows you to measure down from a consistent reference point to gauge the excavation depth and slope.

3 Use 1" (3 cm) dia. outside pipes as gauges for screeding the coarse sand bedding to a consistent thickness that follows the slope you've created.

4 Drag a long, straight 2 × 4 across the screed gauges to strike off the sand at a consistent depth.

4. Pour a layer of coarse sand or sand-based soil into the area so the sand level is slightly above the screed gauges. With a helper, drag a straight 2 × 4 across the screed gauges to level off the sand. Use a screed board that's long enough that you can avoid stepping in the sand. Work the screed in a back-and-forth sawing motion, and remove the screed gauges once each section is finished.

5. Organize your flagstones according to size and appearance. As a general rule of thumb, you should start laying out with your broadest stones and then fill in around them with increasingly smaller flags. But you should also take appearance into account. If you have one nice stone that has an especially flat surface, good color and visual interest, feature it in the center of the patio. Also consider sight lines. If there is an area of the patio that will be visible from the house, for example, or an area that your eye is naturally drawn to by traffic flow, choose your nicer stones for these areas.

6. Begin by laying large, thick flagstones around the perimeter of the patio. Leave a consistent gap between stones by matching pieces like a puzzle and cutting and dressing the stones as needed (see pages 56 to 61).

5 Arrange your flagstones into groups based on size and desirability or shape. This will help you select stones at a glance as your work progresses.

6 Begin laying and leveling large stones around the outer perimeter. If you have a particularly nice stone you'd like to feature as a medallion in the center, position it too. Level the stones by digging under thick areas and packing wet sand under low areas.

Avoid small peninsulas and abrupt irregularities and strive for smooth, curvy edges. To level stones, pry them up with a spud bar and pack wet sand under the low areas.

7. Fill in around the larger stones, working from the outside in. After laying a band of stones three courses wide, re-adjust them to flat. Lay a 2 x 4 across the stones. Move whole stones or just portions of stones up by adding sand beneath. Dig thick portions of stones into the sand base. Dampen the sand occasionally, as this makes it much easier to manipulate and pack. Leave the bedding sand a little lower under the middle of each stone to keep it from rocking.

8. When all of the flags are installed and leveled, rake and sweep a sand-based, weed-seed-free soil (see tip, right) into the cracks and water it'so it settles. Plant plugs or seeds for groundcover to grow up between the stones for a very nice effect. Otherwise, fill the gaps with coarse sand or a decorative gravel such as crushed granite.

Sand-based Soil

Buy sand-based soil in bulk or bags. Also called patio planting soil, it can be found or custom-mixed at most larger garden centers. It is a good material for filling cracks because it is dry and smooth enough to sweep into cracks but will contain enough black compost to support plant growth. Do not use soil from your yard, as it will undoubtedly contain many weed seeds.

7 Fill in around larger stones with smaller stones that have been cut to conform to the openings. Try not to leave any gaps wider than 1" (3 cm), but do not allow stones to touch one another at any point. Use a 2 x 4 guide to check that stones are level as you work.

8 Fill the gaps between stones. You can use sand or mortar mix or just about any kind of granular material you choose. Sand-based soil makes a very effective planting medium (see tip above).

Mortared Flagstone Patio

The stately flagstone patio can be set in mortar for stability and created with lightly trimmed stone or naturally irregular stone shapes. In a mortared patio, smaller stones can be incorporated without the decline in stability that results when they're used in a send-set patio. A classic element of modern landscape design, the Bluestone patio (left) is a very popular stone type, but it may not be available in all areas since specific types vary by region.

When selecting flagstones for your patio project look for consistent color and consistent thickness. Flags in the 2 inch (5 cm) range work well, but because the flags are set into a hard mortar bed you can use thinner rock than you might choose for a sandset patio. You'll need to do quite a bit of cutting and trimming to create flags that fit together neatly, so order at least 25 to 40 percent more square footage in rock than the area of your patio.

You can install a mortared flagstone patio over an old concrete patio if the slab is in reasonably good repair. Or, you can pour a new concrete base that's at least 2-inch (5 cm) thick with a layer of compacted gravel below. You can use any bagged mortar mix you choose for setting the flags. In most building centers you won't even get a choice. But if you do find a choice, purchase either Type N or Type S bagged dry mortar mix.

In the project show here, the gaps between flags are filled with mortar after the patio sets up. If you do this, periodically you will need to remove crumbled mortar and replace it, especially if you live in a moist climate with significant freeze/thaw cycles. Another option that creates a very natural look is to fill the gaps with soil-based sand (see page 119) or peat moss and plant groundcover in the gaps.

TOOLS & MATERIALS

- **Paint roller with extension pole**
- **Pencil**
- **Small whisk broom**
- **Tools for mixing mortar**
- **Shovel**
- **Maul**
- **Stone chisel**
- **Pitching chisel**
- **4-ft. (122 cm) level**
- **Trowel**
- **Straight 2 × 4 stud**
- **Grout bag**
- **Jointing tool**
- **Sponge**
- **Garden hose**
- **Concrete bonding agent**
- **Flagstone stone**
- **Mortar mix**
- **Circular saw with masonry blade**

How to Build a Mortared Flagstone Patio

1. Prepare the concrete slab by fixing large cracks or holes and cleaning thoroughly. Apply concrete bonding agent to the patio surface, following the manufacturer's instructions.

2. Test stone layouts, working from the center outward. Distribute large and stones evenly, with ½ to 1" (13 to 25 mm) joints. Cut stones to size as needed, marking the cutting line with chalk, then cutting the stone. At the sides of the slab, cut stones even with the edges to accommodate edging treatments.

3. Mix a stiff batch of mortar, following the manufacturer's directions. Around the center of the patio, remove the stones and spread a 2"- (5 cm) thick layer of mortar onto the slab. Mix and lay only as much mortar as you can cover with flags in 20 minutes or so.

1 Prepare the concrete base and then apply a coat of bonding adhesive.

2 Dry-lay the flags, marking cutting lines with chalk. Gaps between flags should be ½ to 1" (13 to 25 mm) wide.

3 Lay a bed of mortar for the first flags in the middle of the patio. If weather is hot or dry, dampen the concrete first.

4. Firmly press the first large stone into the mortar, in its same position as in the layout. Tap the stone with a rubber mallet or dead-blow mallet to set it. Use a 4-ft. (122 cm) level and a scrap of 2 × 4 to check for level; make any necessary adjustments.

5. Using the first stone as a reference for the course height, continue to lay stones in mortar, working from the center of the slab to the edges. Maintain even joints. As you work, check for level often. Tap stones to make minor adjustments. Once you're done, let the mortar set up for a day or two before walking on the stones. If necessary, remove stones and add mortar beneath them to raise their length.

6. Use a grout bag to fill the joints with mortar. Pack loose gravel and small rocks into gaps first to conserve mortar and make stronger joints. Once the mortar is stiff enough that your thumb leaves an impression without mortar sticking to it, rake the joints just enough so the mortar is even with the surface of the stone. Use a whisk broom to shape the mortar. Option: After the mortar cures for a week, apply a stone sealer, following the manufacturer's instructions.

4 Set the flags according to your dry-lay pattern. Rap them with a rubber mallet to seat them in the mortar bed.

5 Fill in smaller stones around larger stones, trimming as needed to fit. Make sure stones fit before mortar is applied.

6 Fill a grout bag with mortar and squirt it into the gaps between stones. Rake with a whisk broom. If desired, seal the patio after one week.

Cobblestone Paver Patio

Interlocking stone pavers have advanced by leaps and bounds from the monochromatic, cookie-cutter bricks and slabs associated with first-generation concrete pavers. The latest products feature subtle color blends that lend themselves well to organic, irregular patterns. A tumbling process during manufacturing can further age the pavers so they look more like natural cobblestones. The technological advances in the casting and finishing processes have become so sophisticated that a well-selected concrete paver patio could look as comfortable in a traditional Tuscan village as in a suburban backyard.

When choosing pavers for a patio, pick a style and blend of shapes and sizes that complement your landscape. Use your house and other stone or masonry in the landscape to inform your decisions on colors and shade. Be aware that some paver styles require set purchase amounts, and it's not always possible to return partly used pallets.

Here we lay a cobble patio that uses three sizes of stone. These may be purchased by the band (a fraction of a pallet), minimizing leftovers. Notice that an edge course creates a pleasing border around our patio. Bring a drawing of your patio with exact measurements to your stone yard. Based on your layout pattern, the sales staff will be able to tell you how much of each size stone you'll need to purchase.

One great advantage to interlocking concrete pavers is that they create a very rigid surface with high resistance to movement and sinking, even when set on a gravel base. This makes them suitable for driveways and busy walkways as well as backyard patios. If you prefer, you can set pavers into a mortar bed on a concrete slab.

Note: The differences do not bear on the installation process, but its helpful to distinguish between brick pavers and concrete pavers. Brick pavers are made of fired clay. Concrete pavers are cast from concrete that's placed in forms and cured. Natural cobblestones are small stones with flat, smooth surfaces.

TOOLS & MATERIALS

- Wheelbarrow
- Garden rake
- 4-ft. (122 cm) level
- Hand maul
- Small pry bar
- Wood stakes
- Chalkline
- Mason's string
- Line level
- Tape measure
- Square nose spade
- 1"-dia. (3 cm) metal pipes

- Straight 2 × 4
- 4 × 4 squares of plywood
- Gloves
- Particle mask
- Plate compactor (rental)
- Water-cooled masonry saw (rental)
- Gloves, ear protection and safety glasses
- Stiff bristle broom
- 30% of field: 6 × 6 (15 × 15 cm) cobble squares

- 70% of field: 6 × 9 (15 × 23 cm) cobble rectangles
- 3 × 6 (8 × 15 cm) cobble rectangles for edges
- Compactable gravel base material
- Coarse sand
- Paver edging and spikes
- Joint sand

Cobblestone Paver Patio

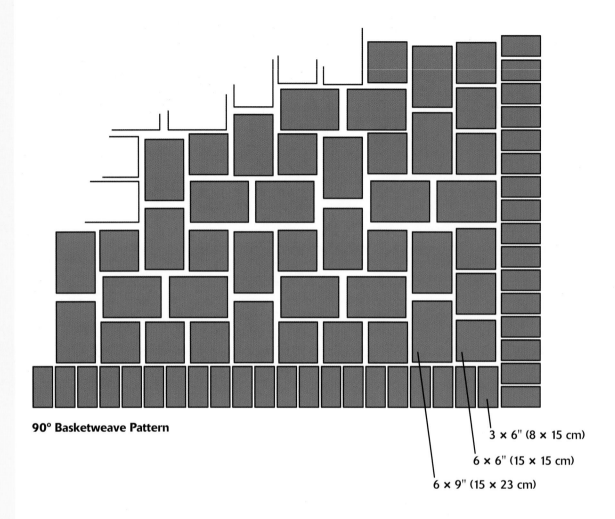

90° Basketweave Pattern

3 × 6" (8 × 15 cm)

6 × 6" (15 × 15 cm)

6 × 9" (15 × 23 cm)

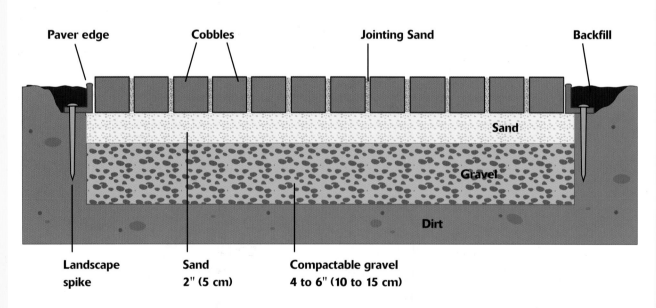

Paver edge **Cobbles** **Jointing Sand** **Backfill**

Sand

Gravel

Dirt

Landscape spike

Sand 2" (5 cm)

Compactable gravel 4 to 6" (10 to 15 cm)

A STURDY PATIO made with interlocking cobbles (pavers) relies on a solid bed made of compactable gravel and sand.

How to Build a Cobblestone Paver Patio

1. Draw your patio to scale on graph paper, after taking careful measurements of the site. Call your state's utility hotline to have service providers mark locations of wires and pipes. Mark the outline for the patio and set mason's lines and grade stakes to a flat or crowned plane that slopes about 1" per 8 ft. (3 cm per 2.4 m) for drainage. All drainage slopes should be away from building foundations.

2. Excavate to a depth that accommodates 4" (10 cm) of compactable base material, a ¾" (19 mm)-thick layer of sand (after compaction), and the thickness of the pavers. Extend the excavated area at least 6" (15 cm) beyond the patio edges. If you have soft or clayey soil, install 8" (20 cm) of base material instead of 4" (10 cm). Using a plate compactor, compress the soil after you excavate but before you spread the base material.

3. Create a 4" (10 cm)-thick compacted gravel base foundation that maintains the drainage pitch. Once you have poured the compactable gravel into the project area, use a straight 2 × 4 to rake the material so it is smooth and follows the depth guide created by the string layouts. Fill low spots deeper than ¼" (6 mm) beneath the 2 × 4. Check for drainage pitch by putting a level on top of the 2 × 4. The base surface should be below finished patio level by ¾" (19 mm), plus the thickness of your pavers. Err on the side of too high where the patio meets he lawn or garden—it's better to grade up to the patio than have lawns and gardens drain onto the patio surface. Remove grade stakes and then compact thoroughly with a plate compactor.

1 Lay out the patio outline and set digging depth with grade stakes. Factor a minimum 1" per 8 ft. (3 cm per 2.4 m) of drainage slope away from the house if the patio is next to your home. Remove the strings.

2 Excavate the building site, paying close attention to the outlines and stakes that denote the excavation depth and slope.

3 Rake and screed the compactable gravel to follow the drainage slope and then compact with a plate compactor.

Paver edge spikes

4 Lay out square corners for the patio with stakes and string, starting next to an adjoining structure. Use the 3-4-5 method to check the intersecting lines for squareness at the corners.

5 Snap chalklines directly below the outlines you've created with the mason's strings and then install professional-grade paver edging at the lines. The paver edge should rest on compacted gravel, not soil.

6 Strike off the coarse sand base by dragging a 2 × 4 screed across 1" (3 cm) pipes that are used as screed gauges.

4. Drive stakes and tie mason's lines to establish two square edges of your patio. Start at a straight building or driveway for your base line, if applicable, but don't assume these structures are straight. Rather, pull a line along the structure that remains equal to or less than an edge-block length away from the structure. Measure three units along one line and four along the next and mark these points. When a measuring tape drawn between these points equals five units, your lines are square.

5. Snap a chalkline directly onto your compacted base along the line following the unsupported edge. Remove the mason's strings. Set the rigid plastic paver edge up against the chalkline. Drive the edge spikes part way in, in case you need to move the edging.

6. Lay lengths of metal pipe in the project area at to serve as screed gauges. Fill the patio area with coarse building sand and then screed the sand with a straight 2 × 4, working outward from your square corner. For best results, use a long 2 × 4 and have a helper work one end of the screed. Always pull sand toward yourself over screeding. Overlap old pipes with new as needed. Remove pipes as they are no longer needed and fill the channels with sand.

7. Reset your line along your house, near ground level. Lay cobbles in your chosen pattern from the square corner formed by this base line and the set edge. Start with edge stones along the plastic paver edge, but begin setting your field stones directly from the string along the house. Later, you will cut edge stones to fit against the edge of the foundation, which can be uneven. Stones should never be shuffled sideways in the sand or pounded down; the plate compactor will flatten them later.

7 Begin laying out the cobbles, starting at the square corner. Work in small sections on approximately 5 square ft. (1.5 m). Simply set the cobbles into the sand base—do not adjust them from side to side or try to re-set the height.

Creating a Layout

The number of purchasing options available when you shop for pavers makes it possible to create just about any patio layout pattern you can imagine. There is nothing stopping you from going wild and creating a layout that's truly creative. However, most landscape centers are happy to work with you to create a layout that employs tested design ideas and consumes pavers in a very efficient manner with as little cutting as possible.

Another option for DIY designers is to visit the website of the paver manufacturer (you should be able to get the information from your paver dealer). Many of these have applications where you can choose a basic style you like (such as the basketweave pattern seen here), enter in some size information. You'll receive a printout of what the pattern should look like, along with a shopping list for the materials you'll need, all the way down to sand and spikes for your paver edging. To see an example of a design calculator/estimator, visit the Website for Borgert Products, maker of the cobbles seen here in a 30% square, 70% rectangle basketweave pattern with rectangular border (see Resources, page 172).

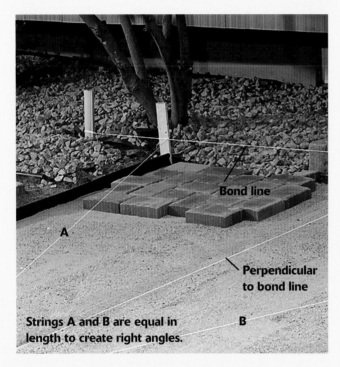

Bond line

A

Perpendicular to bond line

Strings A and B are equal in length to create right angles.

B

Bond line

Paver edging

8 Tie additional strings to establish a guide line that bisects the project and is perpendicular to the bond line at the end of the layout pattern.

9 Install the paver edging for the rest of the patio, using the bond lines as reference. Brush sand out of the edging installation area so the paver edging rests on the compactable base. Replace and smooth the sand after the edging is installed.

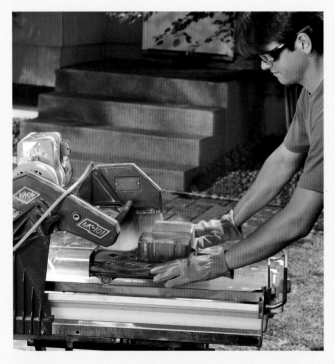

10 Cut the cobbles to fit the layout using a wet saw (rentable). See page 58 for more information on cutting pavers.

11 Fill gaps between cobbles with decorative sand, such as crushed granite, or with specially formulated jointing sand that hardens when dampened for a more formal look.

8. Set a line perpendicular to your base line, following a bond line at the edge of the patio. Use this line to make sure your bond lines aren't drifting. You can loosen joints to adjust pavers to the line with a small pry bar. If you can't keep to a line because it's too tight to the edge, adjust the line or edge, whichever is not square. Set new lines about every 4 ft. (1.2 m) so you are never laying very far from a line.

9. A straight patio edge must fall on a bond line created by the last field stone edge plus the length of an edge stone. Add a little space for wiggle room. String a line just over the sand at the inside position of the edge. Cut away the sand beyond this line and set your paver edge on the base material. Drive stakes in partially. Smooth sand as needed.

10. Fill in the remaining whole pavers in the layout and then cut pavers to fit as your layout dictates. It's preferable to cut pavers a little too small than to have very tight fits. The joint sand will fill small gaps. Cut the cobbles with a rented wet saw, keeping well away from the installation area—the stream of slurry kicked out by the wet saw as it cuts can stain the surfaces of the placed pavers.

11. Sweep coarse dry sand, such as crushed granite, into the joints. Or, use a specially formulated joint sand that sets when it gets wet (see Resources, page 172).

12. Run a gas-powered plate compactor in a circular pattern from the outside in, in overlapping rings. Do not skimp on this step by substituting a hand tamper. Your patio will not be flat and you will run a greater risk of damaging cobbles. Sweep more sand into the joints and compact again. Repeat as needed until no more sand can be added. Once you're done compacting, sweep excess gap-filler material off the patio and water the surfaces to help material settle.

Making Curves

At rounded corners and curves, install border pavers (top photo) in a fan pattern with even gaps between the pavers. Gentle curves may accommodate full-size border pavers, but for sharper turns you usually need to cut tapers into the paver edges so you don't end up with wide gaps at the outside. When using border pavers in a curved layout, the filed pavers will need to be trimmed to fit the odd spaces created where the filed and borders intersect (bottom photo).

12 Tamp the cobble stones with a plate compactor to bring them to level and seat them in the base. Add jointing sand in the joints if levels drop as you work.

Stone Firepit

A fire pit makes a wonderful focal point for backyard gatherings. Many local codes stipulate that the pit area should be at least 20 feet (6 m) across, including the surrounding circular area that can be outfitted with chairs and benches. Dressed with rock (trap rock is shown here), this area creates a firebreak between the pit and structures or flammable yard elements, such as landscape plants and dry lawns. For comfort and safety, firepits should only be installed on level ground. If your proposed seating area is on a slope, you can build a retaining wall (see pages 140 to 147) on the high side, providing another surface for seating or setting down plates and drinks.

The firepit featured here is constructed around a metal liner, available from landscape supply centers. A liner will keep the fire pit walls from overheating and cracking if cooled suddenly by rain or a bucket of water. The liner seen here is a section of 36-inch (91 cm)-diameter corrugated culvert pipe.

This firepit is built with ashlar wall stones. You may use any type of stone you prefer, including cast concrete retaining wall blocks. Set the stones on a solid foundation of compactable gravel, just as you'd set a wall or paver patio. We recommend you prep the base for the seating area at the same time as the fire pit, so both rest on the same level plane.

Most municipalities regulate the allowable size of a residential firepit, as well as minimum distances from structures and other flammable landscape elements. Some also may require that you obtain a permit each time you use the firepit, or at least that you notify your local fire department so responders aren't dispatched unnecessarily.

Here are a few pointers to consider once you are ready to use your firepit:
- Make sure there are no bans or restrictions in effect.
- Evaluate wind conditions. Do not build a fire if winds are heavy, especially if they are blowing toward your home.
- Keep shovels, sand and a supply of water nearby. A fire extinguisher is also recommended.
- Extinguish the fire with water and do not leave it unattended until it is cold to the touch.

TOOLS & MATERIALS

- Wheelbarrow
- Landscape paint
- String and stakes
- Spades
- Metal pipe
- Landscape edging
- Metal firepit liner
- Compactable gravel
- Top-dressing rock (trap rock)
- Wall stones

Stone Firepit

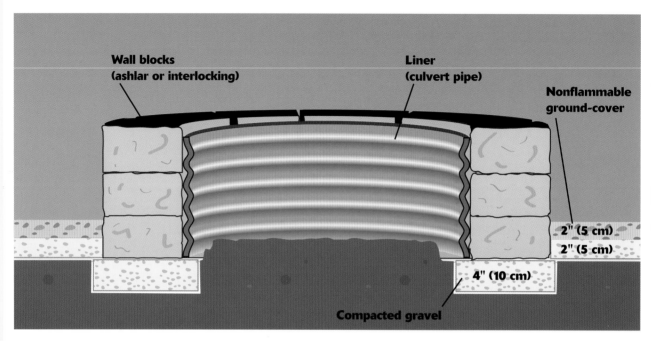

Wall blocks (ashlar or interlocking)

Liner (culvert pipe)

Nonflammable ground-cover

2" (5 cm)

2" (5 cm)

4" (10 cm)

Compacted gravel

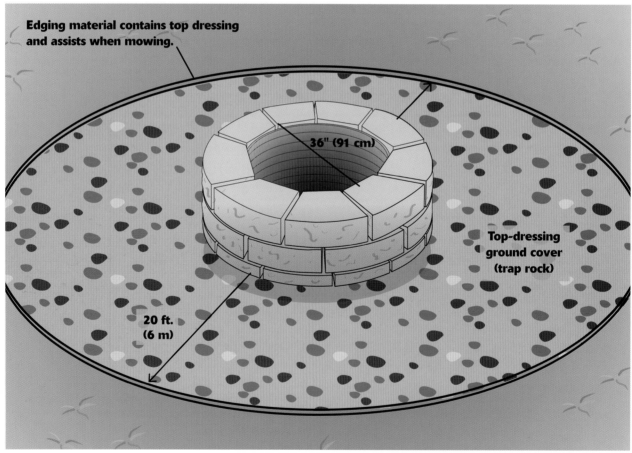

Edging material contains top dressing and assists when mowing.

36" (91 cm)

Top-dressing ground cover (trap rock)

20 ft. (6 m)

A STONE FIREPIT is made from ashlar wall block stacked around a metal pit liner. The trap-rock dressing surrounding the pit protects against fire from sparks and provides a comfortable seating area.

How to Make a Firepit

1. Call your local utilities hotline to have service providers mark locations of underground pipes and wires. Locate your firepit area away from trees, wires, buildings, and areas where flammable materials are stored. Check your local fire codes regarding specifics of firepit use in your area (see page 135). Drive a length of pipe into the center of the pit area. Measure out two distances from the pipe: the first marks the outside radius of the firepit; the second marks the outside radius of your seating area. Use a cord with a loop in it and a can of landscape marking paint to draw circles with these radii on the ground around the pipe. Determine if the distance between the two circles in sufficient for safe, comfortable seating.

2. If you are satisfied with the size of the seating area, cut out the sod and excavate to a level plane 4" (10 cm) below grade for the entire circled area, from pipe to perimeter. Leave your center pipe in place. Add edging at the perimeter of the seating area. Drive stakes and mark them within depth lines.

3. Re-draw the firepit circle from the center pipe. Add an extra 6" (15 cm) to the radius. Now draw the inner circumference of the firepit minus 6" (15 cm). These lines mark a broad base to support the fire-pit stones. Excavate an additional 4" (10 cm) down within this ring and compact the soil at the bottom of this trench with a hand tamper.

1 Outline the location for your firepit and the firepit safety area by drawing concentric circles with landscape paint, using a string and pole for guidance.

2 Remove a 4" (10 cm)-deep layer of sod and dirt in the firepit and safety areas (the depth of the excavation depends on what materials you're installing in the safety zone.)

3 Dig a 4" (10 cm)-deep trench for the perimeter stones that will ring the pit liner.

4 Fill the trench for the perimeter stones with compactable gravel and tamp thoroughly. Then scatter gravel to within 2½" (8 cm) of the paver edging top throughout the project area. It is not necessary to tamp this layer at this time.

5 Place your metal fire ring so it is level on the gravel layer and centered around the center pipe.

6 Arrange the first course of wall blocks around the fire ring. Keep gaps even and check with a level, adding or removing gravel as needed.

4. Completely fill the trench with compactable gravel and compact with a hand tamper until it is very hard. Fill the entire area (pit and seating/safety) with compactable gravel to 2" (5 cm) below grade. Use a level on a straight 2 x 4 to assist in flattening the gravel. The area beneath the pit in particular must be perfectly flat and level. Do not compact the top layer of gravel.

5. Center the metal firepit liner around the center pipe and level it on top of the loose compactable gravel.

6. Lay your first course of wall stones around the liner. Adjust the stones so they maintain a consistent spacing to the liner and between one another.

7. Remove the center pipe and lay the second course of wall stones. Stagger the vertical joints of the first and second courses. Do not use landscape block adhesive to bond the courses together, as you would for a retaining wall. It is not heat-resistant. Add additional courses, including a cap row of smooth, flat stones, until the height of the stones exceeds the height of the liner.

8. Compact the gravel in the seating/safety area with a plate compactor. This will stabilize the area and also help create a hard subbase that inhibits weed growth.

9. Lay and rake smooth a 2" (5 cm) layer of decorative top-dressing rock in the seating area. Compact with the plate compactor after grading to flat and level. The compaction will help make the surface easier to walk upon. An angular rock, such as the trap rock seen here, makes a better walking surface than smooth gravel.

7 Install the second course of retaining all block, taking care to evenly stagger the vertical joints on the first and second courses. Add the remaining courses.

8 Compact the compactable gravel in the seating/safety area, using a rental plate vibrator.

9 Place and compact a layer of top-dressing rock in the seating/safety area to complete the firepit.

Stone Retaining Wall

Rough-cut wall stones may be dry stacked (without mortar) into retaining walls, garden walls and other stonescape features. Dry-stack walls are able to move and shift with the frost, and they also drain well so they don't require deep footings and drainage tiles. Unlike fieldstone and boulder walls, short wall-stone walls can be just a single stone thick.

In the project featured here, we use rough-split limestone blocks about 8 inch by about 4 inch (20 × 10 cm) thick and in varying lengths. Walls like this may be built up to 3 feet tall, but keep them shorter if you can, to be safe. Building multiple short walls is often a more effective way to manage a slope than to build one taller wall. Called terracing, this practice requires some planning. Ideally, the flat ground between pairs of walls will be approximately the uniform size.

A dry-laid natural stone retaining wall is a very organic looking structure compared to interlocking block retaining walls (see pages 148 to 149). One way to exploit the natural look is to plant some of your favorite stone-garden perennials in the joints as you build the wall(s). Usually one plant or a cluster of three will add interest to a wall without suffocating it in vegetation or compromising its stability. Avoid plants that get very large or develop thick, woody roots or stems that may compromise the stability of the wall.

A well-built retaining wall has a slight lean, called a batter, back into the slope. It has a solid base and the bottom course is dug in behind the lower terrace. Drainage gravel can help keep the soil from turning to mud, which will slump and press against the wall.

The same basic techniques used to stack natural stone in a retaining wall may be used for building a short garden wall as well. Obviously, there is no need for drainage allowances or wall returns in a garden wall. Simply prepare a base similar to the one shown here and begin stacking. The wall will look best if it wanders and meanders a bit. Unless you're building a very short wall (less than 18 inches [46 cm]) use two parallel courses that lean against one another for the basic construction. Cap it with flat capstones that run the full width of the wall (see page 155).

TOOLS & MATERIALS

- **Goggles, gloves, steel-toe boots**
- **Mattock with pick**
- **Hatchet or loppers**
- **Spades**
- **Measuring tape**
- **Mason's string**

- **Line level**
- **Stakes**
- **Hand maul**
- **Torpedo level**
- **Straight 2 × 4**
- **Hand tamper**
- **Compactable gravel**

- **Ashlar wall stone**
- **Drainage gravel**
- **Landscape fabric**
- **Block and stone adhesive**
- **Caulk gun**

Stone Retaining Wall

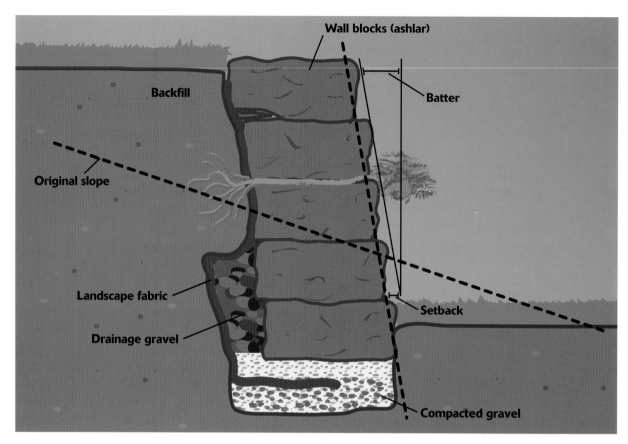

Wall blocks (ashlar)

Backfill

Batter

Original slope

Landscape fabric

Drainage gravel

Setback

Compacted gravel

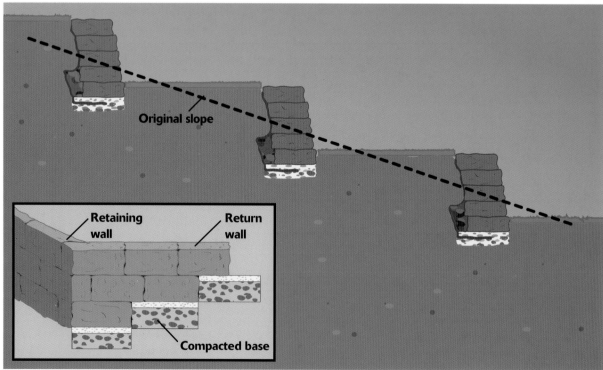

Original slope

Retaining wall

Return wall

Compacted base

A STONE RETAINING WALL breaks up a slope to neat flat lawn areas that are more usable (top). A series of walls and terraces (bottom) break up larger slopes. Short return walls (inset) create transitions to the yard.

How to Build a Stone Retaining Wall

1. Call your local utilities hotline to have area checked for buried pipes and wires. Lay out the path of the wall or walls with stakes and string. See pages 22 to 23 for more information. Dig back into the slope, creating your first level terrace. For a 2 ft. (61 cm) wall, you'll remove at least one vertical foot of the slope. Slope the back of your excavation to roughly follow the batter of your retaining wall. Your wall will stand at least 6" (15 cm) in front of the cut to make room for drainage gravel. Dig returns back into the slope at each end of the retaining wall, terminating them where they become too deep.

2. Excavate a base trench 8" (20 cm) below grade for the main wall and the returns. Make it wider than your stones by at least 3" (8 cm), back and front. Level the trench bottom lengthwise by measuring down from a level string. If the trench becomes too shallow, step it down the height of one stone.

3. Tamp the soil in the trench and then tamp 3" (8 cm) of compactable gravel into the trench. Drape landscape fabric over this base and up the back of the excavation. Add a 1" (3 cm) layer of coarse sand and level it back to front and side to side. Use a long and a short length of 2 × 4 as a screeding/leveling tool. Use a torpedo level to check the 2 × 4s for level. All points of your base must remain below the level of the lower terrace.

1 Dig into the slope to create a trench for the first wall. Reserve the soil you remove nearby—you'll want to backfill with it when the wall is done.

2 Level the bottom of the trench and measure to make sure you've excavated deeply enough.

3 After compacting a base, cover the trench and hill slope with landscape fabric then pour and level a 1" (3 cm) layer of coarse sand.

4 Place the first course of stones in rough position. Run a level mason's string at the average height of the stones.

4. Organize your stones so that each course may be made with stones of similar thickness. Set aside some large, long stones for the top course (cap stones). Set your first course with heavy stones, laying long, square-ended stones at the corners first. Draw a level string just in front of the top front of the course, letting the stones roughly guide the string placement.

5. Add or remove sand beneath the stones as needed so they all are at or very close to the mason's string height. Set stones should not touch the line. Level the stones back to front with a torpedo level and side-to-side with a 4-ft. (122 cm) level. Use a hand maul and a stone chisel to chip off the occasional irregularity, but don't get too carried away.

6. Reset your level line to the approximate height of the stones you will use in the next course, but put it ½" (13 mm) closer to the slope. This setback will be repeated on every course to create the batter. Lay the corner stones of the second course first. Alternate the orientation of the long stones between the return and the main wall so that they interlock. Choose face stones so vertical joints don't line up. Use stone chips as shims if needed to stabilize the stones and help with level.

5 Add or remove gravel under each stone to bring the front edges level with the mason's string.

6 Begin the second course with a longer stone on each end so the vertical gaps between stones are staggered over the first course.

7. Complete the second course, using shards or cut pieces of stone as shims to level the individual stones. Make sure to maintain a ½" (13 mm) setback from the first course to establish the right batter.

8. Add stones to create the return as need. Often, you'll need to dig out slightly in order to have the return stones be level with the other stones in the course. Make sure you place a layer of compactable gravel under each return

9. Backfill immediately with drainage rock (not compactable gravel) between the retaining wall and the fabric-covered excavation. Rounded stones like river rock in 1½ to 3" (4 to 8 cm) diameters make good drainage rock because they don't knit together like more angular rocks. Pack the gravel in with the end of a 2 × 4 to help it settle.

Tip: Drainage tile is sometimes recommended for installation behind dry-stacked stone retaining walls. Inquire at your land-scape materials supplier to find out if it is advisable for your wall.

7 Finish out the second course. Use shards and chips of stone as shims where needed to stabilize the stones. Check to make sure the ½" (3 mm) setback is followed.

8 Finish setting the return stones in the second course, making adjustments as needed for the return to be level.

9 Backfill behind the wall with river rock or another good drainage rock.

10 Fold the landscape fabric over the drainage rock (the main job of the fabric is to keep soil from migrating into the drainage rock and out the wall) and backfill behind it with soil to level the ground.

11 Trim the landscape fabric just behind the back of the wall, near the top.

12 Finish the wall by capping it off with some of your nicer, long flat stones. Bond them with block-and-stone adhesive.

10. Fold the landscape fabric over the top of the river rock backfill. Add soil to backfill the area behind the wall until it is level with the wall top.

11. Once you've backfilled with dirt all the way to the top of the wall, trim the landscape fabric so it is just below the top of the wall in the back, using scissors.

12. Adhere a cap course of long, flat stones to the last course, using block-and-stone adhesive. Backfill further to within an inch of the top of the wall with soil.

13. Level and rake the soil behind the retaining wall, amending it with fertilizers as needed if you will be planting it. Build additional walls in the same manner if you are terracing a larger slope. Do not exceed 3 ft. (91 cm) in height for any walls.

13 Level off the soil behind the wall with a garden rake. Add additional walls if you are terracing.

Planting Your Retaining Wall

Natural stone retaining walls look quite lovely in their own right. However, you can enhance the effect by making some well-chosen planting choices for the wall itself. You can plan for this in the wall construction by leaving an extra wide gap between two stones in one of the courses and then planting in the gap. Or you can replace a stone in the wall with a shorter one, also creating a gap. To plant a gap, cut the fabric and set a good-size bare-root perennial of an appropriate species to the bottom of this joint. Fan out the roots over the soil and use sphagnum moss to plug up the gaps in the wall around plants. Adhere the stone in the next course that bridges the gap with block and stone adhesive. Keep plants well watered until established. Eventually, the plant roots will hold the soil instead of the moss.

Set plants in natural-looking clusters of the same species. Do not suffocate the wall with too many plants.

Interlocking Block Retaining Wall

Retaining walls are often used to level a yard or to prevent erosion on a hillside. In a flat yard, you can build a low retaining wall and fill in behind it to create a raised planting bed. Terraced retaining walls work well on steep hillsides. Two or more short retaining walls are easier to install and more stable than a single, tall retaining wall. Construct the terraces so each wall is no higher than 3 ft. (91 cm).

While retaining walls can be built from many materials, including pressure-treated timbers and natural stone, interlocking concrete blocks have become a very popular choice. Typically made from concrete, interlocking retaining wall blocks are rather inexpensive, very durable, and DIY-friendly. Several styles of interlocking block are available at building centers and landscape materials suppliers. Most types have a split-face finish that combines the rough texture of cut stone with the uniform shape and size of concrete blocks. Some have cast flanges or tongues and grooves to create a mechanical bond that holds the walls together. Other types do not interlock, but have flat surfaces that need to be bonded with rock and stone adhesive. Some older styles relied on nylon pins that fit into cast holes in the blocks to add strength and assist in alignement. These fasteners are no longer widely available.

Interlocking block weighs up to 80 lbs. (35 kg) each, so it is a good idea to have helpers when building a retaining wall. Suppliers offer substantial discounts when interlocking block is purchased in large quantities, so you may be able to save money if you coordinate your own project with those of your neighbors.

Structural features for all retaining walls include: a compactable gravel subbase to make a solid footing for the wall, crushed stone backfill and a perforated drain pipe to improve drainage behind the wall, and landscape fabric to keep the loose soil from washing into and clogging the gravel backfill.

When building retaining walls, pay special attention to drainage. Your wall can be damaged if water saturates the soil behind it, so make sure you include the proper drainage gravel and drain pipes or tile. You may need to dig a drainage swale before building in low-lying areas.

Be sure to check your local codes for maximum wall height restrictions and for minimum property line setback. Also have your public utility company visit your property and flag any utility lines that are in or near the project area.

TOOLS & MATERIALS

- Wheelbarrow
- Shovel
- Garden rake
- Line level
- Hand tamper
- Plate compactor
- 3-lb. maul
- Masonry chisel

- Eye protection
- Hearing protection
- Work gloves
- Circular saw with masonry blade
- Level
- Tape measure
- Marking pencil

- Caulk gun
- Stakes
- Mason's string
- Landscape fabric
- Compactable gravel
- Perforated drain tile
- Backfill gravel
- Construction adhesive

Options for Positioning a Retaining Wall

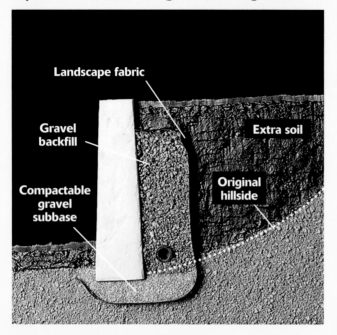

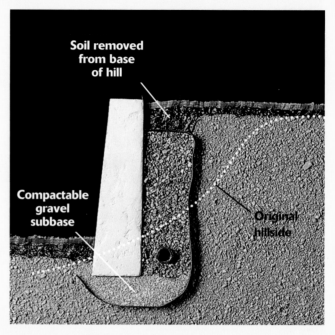

Increase the level area above the wall by positioning the wall well forward from the top of the hill. Fill in behind the wall with extra soil, which is available from sand-and-gravel companies.

Keep the basic shape of your yard by positioning the wall near the top of the hillside. Use the soil removed at the base of the hill to fill in near the top of the wall.

Tips for Building Retaining Walls

Backfill with crushed stone and install a perforated drain pipe about 6" (15 cm) above the bottom of the backfill. Vent the pipe to the side or bottom of the retaining wall, where runoff water can flow away from the hillside without causing erosion.

Make a stepped trench when the ends of a retaining wall must blend into an existing hillside. Retaining walls often are designed so the ends curve or turn back into the slope.

How to Build an Interlocking Block Retaining Wall

1. Excavate the hillside as necessary. Allow 12" (30 cm) of space for crushed stone backfill between the back of the wall and the hillside. Use stakes to mark the front edge of the wall. Connect the stakes with mason's string, and use a line level to check for level. The base of the trench must always remain at least 6" (15 cm).

2. Line the excavation with strips of landscape fabric cut 3 ft. longer than the planned height of the wall. Make sure all seams overlap by at least 6" (15 cm).

3. Spread a 4" (10 cm) layer of compactable gravel over the bottom of the excavation as a subbase and pack it thoroughly. A rented plate compactor works better than a hand tamper for packing the subbase. The compacted base must be flat in order for the wall to be level, so check it frequently with a level.

1 Lay out the wall location with stakes and string and excavate as needed.

2 Line the trench with landscape fabric and pin or stake it temporarily at the highpoint.

3 Place a 4" (10 cm)-thick layer of compactable gravel in the trench and compact it with a plate compactor.

4 Begin laying the first course. Check for level frequently.

4. Lay the first course of block, aligning the front edges with the mason's string. When using flanged block, some manufacturers recommend that you place the first course upside down and backward. Check frequently with a level and adjust, if necessary, by adding or removing subbase material below the blocks.

5. Lay the second course of block according to manufacturer's instructions, checking to make sure the blocks are level. Lay flanged block with the flanges tight against the underlying course. Add 3 to 4" (8 to 10 cm) of gravel behind the block, and pack it with a hand tamper.

6. Make half-blocks for the corners and ends of a wall, and use them to stagger vertical joints between courses. Score full blocks with a circular saw and masonry blade, then break the blocks along the scored line with a maul and chisel.

Note: Some manufacturers sell precast half-blocks so you do not have to create your own.

5 Lay the second course of block on top of the starter course making sure the vertical seams are staggered. Backfill with drainage rock as you work.

6 Cut half-blocks for corners on alternating courses.

7. Add and tamp crushed stone, as needed, to create a slight downward pitch (about ¼" [6 mm] of height per foot [30 cm]) leading to the drain pipe outlet. Place the drain pipe on the crushed stone, 6" (15 cm) behind the wall, with the perforations face down. Make sure the pipe outlet is unobstructed. Lay courses of block until the wall is about 18" (46 cm) above ground level, staggering the vertical joints. Fill behind the wall with crushed stone, and pack it with the hand tamper. Lay the remaining courses of block, except for the cap row, backfilling with crushed stone and packing with the tamper as you go.

8. Before laying the cap block, fold the end of the landscape fabric over the crushed stone backfill. Add a thin layer of topsoil over the fabric, then pack it thoroughly with a hand tamper. Fold any excess landscape fabric back over the tamped soil.

9. Apply stone and rock adhesive to the top course of block, then lay the cap blocks. Use topsoil to fill in behind the wall and to fill in the base at the front of the wall. Install sod or plants, as desired.

7 Lay perforated drain pipe at a slight slope behind the wall and cover with drainage rock.

8 Fold the landscape fabric back against the drainage rock and then backfill over the fabric with black dirt.

9 Install the wall cap blocks using stone and rock adhesive if recommended by the manufacturer.

Stone Garden Wall

Many homeowners—especially dedicated gardeners—dream of using low stone walls to form the boundaries of their yards or gardens. Sadly, many of them think those stone walls are destined to remain merely dreams. If you're one of those people, you'll be happy to hear that you don't have to hire a mason to build a durable stone wall.

You can construct a low stone wall without a concrete footing and only a little mortar using a centuries-old method known as "dry-laying." The wall is formed by two separate stacks, called wythes, that lean in on each other. When the ground shifts under the wall (as it will), the stones shift with them—there is no monolithic hunk of masonry to crack and crumble because of the movement.

While dry walls are simple, they do require patience and a strong back. Heavy stones must be carefully selected, sorted, and applied in the wall so each course runs level and the wall fits together well. We recommend you use a sedimentary block stone like the limestone we use here. The rectangular shapes and parallel striations make them natural building blocks. Plus, sedimentary stones are relatively easy to cut and split. We suggest a masonry blade in a circular saw to score the stones if needed and a stone chisel and hand sledge to split them. Wear eye and ear protection.

If you do choose to build a wall out of more rounded fieldstones, plan on a wider wall with more pronounced butter (*lead*) to the opposing sides. The gap between the sides (*wythes*) will get smaller as the wall grows up. Fill this gap with rubble stones. A cap stone may be used with a dry-laid fieldstone wall.

TOOLS & MATERIALS

- Shovel
- Circular saw with masonry blade
- Hand maul
- Masonry chisel
- 4-ft. (122 cm) level
- Masonry trowel
- Safety glasses
- Stones of various shapes and sizes
- Capstone
- Bagged mortar mix
- Rough-textured rag
- Line level
- Folding rule
- Compactable gravel base

Choosing Stones

For this wall, you'll need stones in four general categories.

Shaping: half or less as wide as the wall and any length. Sedimentary rock is sold in relatively consistent widths and variable lengths. Longer shaping stones make for a more stable wall.

Tie: These are stones that are as long as the wall is wide.

Filler: Also called rubble, these are small and irregular fragments that fit into cracks and fill the spaces between the wythes.

Cap: These are large, flat stones, sometimes called flags that are wider than the top of your wall.

Sort the stones by size and purpose, placing them in piles near the building site.

This kind of wall must be at least half as wide as it is tall, and the wall must have a batter, that is, it must get narrower as it goes up. The wall we build here didn't need much of a batter because of the regularity of the stones, but walls of less even stones need a considerable inward lean to stay standing as the ground shifts during freeze/thaw cycles. This requires spacing the lower wythes farther apart and filling the gap with rubble.

We use mortar on the capstones to keep these from being knocked off. Some of these mortar joints will break over time, but this shouldn't compromise the overall strength or beauty of the wall.

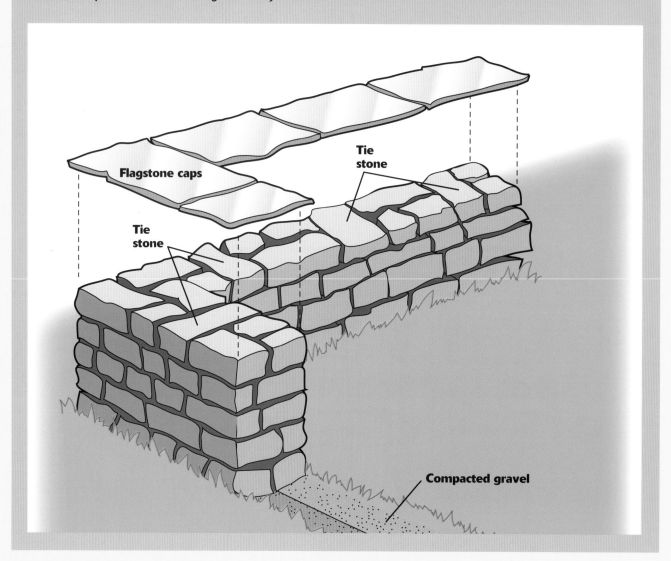

How to Build a Dry-stack Stone Wall

1. Outline and dig a 24" (61 cm) wide trench within your outside fence line. You can widen this if you have large stones or need more of a batter. Set a level mason's line above the trench, and keep the bottom of the trench a consistent distance below the line. Deepen your trench to a minimum of 6" (15 cm) at the sides and 8" (20 cm) in the middle. The sides should be vertical. Compact loose soil with a hand tamper. Line the trench with 2" (5 cm) of compactable gravel sub-base. Do not compact this base.

2. Begin laying pairs of parallel stones in two rows along the bottom of the trench. Position them flush with the edges of the trench and sloping in toward the center. If you have a corner, start there, meshing the intersecting walls together. Place the uneven sides of your stones down in the gravel and push or dig them in. Your two rows may have a gap in the center, which you need to fill with rubble stone. Level individual stones front to back. Use a 4 ft. (122 cm) level to keep the stones within a wythe level and to keep the wythes level with each other. As you approach the end, cut stones as needed, but use long stones for the very end.

3. Use large, long evenly shaped stones at the corners of the second course. Overlap the stones of the meeting walls in a way that ties the walls together. Work down the line, staggering the joints. You may shim and space stones as needed with stone fragments.

1 Dig a trench. As you deepen it, make the sides vertical, but create a V-shaped dip in the bottom. Keep the trench a consistent distance below a level mason's line.

2 Set your first course in a bed of gravel. Tie your corners together.

3 Use stone fragments to fill gaps and level your stones. Long stones overlapping at corners help stabilize the wall.

QUICK TIP: CURVED WALLS

To build a curved wall, lay out the curve using a string staked to a center point, and dig the trench and set stones as for a straight wall. Lay the stones as for a straight wall, but use shorter stones; long, horizontal stones do not work as well for a tight curve. Lay the stones so they are tight together, off-setting the joints along the entire stretch. Be careful to keep the stone faces vertical to sustain the curve all the way up the height of the wall.

4. You may need tie stones across the width of the wall near the corners and ends; otherwise, only use parallel shaping stones on the second course. Each consecutive wall course should be slightly narrower then the one below, causing the wall faces to slope inward. Use long shaping stones at the end of the wall, cutting the stones preceding those if needed. Continue each course, tying corners together with long overlapping stones and using long stones toward the wall ends. Every third course, use tie stones across the width of the wall to hold the wythes together. Space these every 3 ft. (91 cm) or so.

5. Apply a stiff mortar to the top blocks far enough from the stone faces that it will be concealed. Level the capstones on the tops. Use slivers of stone for shims.

   Clean mortar off the stone faces with a damp rag and a brush before it cures.

4 Every other course, place a full-width tie stone at 3 ft. (91 cm) intervals. Check the wall for level as you work.

5 Bond the flagstone cap stones to the top of the wall with mortar or with brick and stone adhesive. Do not apply mortar near the edges—the wall looks better if mortar can't be seen.

Variation: Mortared Stone Wall

The classic look of a mortared stone wall adds a sense of solidity and permanence to a landscape that nothing else can match. Although building a mortared wall takes more work than building a dry-laid one, the tailored look of mortared stone may be just what's needed. Plan and position your wall carefully—making changes requires a sledgehammer and a fair amount of sweat.

Before you begin work, check local building codes for regulations regarding the size and depth of the required concrete footings as well as construction details. And remember, in most communities any building project that requires a footing requires a building permit.

Plan to make your wall no more than 18" (46 cm) wide. Purchase a generous supply of stone so that you have plenty to choose from as you fit the wall together. Laying stone is much like putting a jigsaw puzzle together, and the pieces must fit well enough that gravity and their weight—rather than the strength of the mortar—will hold the wall together. Your stone supplier can help you calculate the tonnage necessary for your project, but you can make rough estimates with these formulas:

Ashlar: The area of the wall face (sq. ft.) divided by 15 equals the number of tons needed.

Rubble: The area of the wall face (sq. ft.) divided by 35 equals the number of tons necessary.

PACK VOIDS between wall stones with mortar and stone shards.

TRIM CAP STONES to fit and set them into a thick mortar bed.

Arroyo

An arroyo is a dry stream bed or watercourse in an arid climate that directs water runoff on the rare occasions when there is a downfall. In a home landscape an arroyo may be used for purely decorative purposes, with the placement of stones evoking water where the real thing is scarce. Or it may serve a vital water-management function, directing storm runoff away from building foundations to areas where it may percolate into the ground and irrigate plants, creating a great spot for a rain garden. This water management function is becoming more important as municipalities struggle with an overload of storm sewer water, which can degrade water quality in rivers and lakes. Some communities now offer tax incentives to homeowners who keep water out of the street.

When designing your dry streambed, keep it natural and practical. Use local stone that's arranged as it would be found in a natural stream. Take a field trip to an area containing natural streams and make some observations. Note how quickly the water depth drops at the outside of bends where only larger stones can withstand the current. By the same token, note how gradually the water level drops at the inside of broad bends where water movement is slow. Place smaller river-rock gravel here, as it would accumulate in a natural stream.

Large heavy stones with flat tops may serve as step stones, allowing paths to cross or even follow dry stream beds.

The most important design standard with dry streambeds is to avoid regularity. Stones are never spaced evenly in nature nor should they be in your arroyo. If you dig a bed with consistent width it will look like a canal or a drainage ditch, not a stream. And consider other yard elements and furnishings. For example, an arroyo presents a nice opportunity to add a landscape bridge or two to your yard.

Important: Contact your local government before deliberately routing water toward a storm sewer; this may be illegal.

TOOLS & MATERIALS

- Landscape paint
- Carpenters level
- Spades
- Garden rake
- Wheelbarrow
- Landscape fabric
- 6-mil black plastic
- Mulch
- 6 to 18" dia. (15 to 46 cm) river-rock boulders
- 8" (20 cm)-thick steppers
- ¾ to 2" (19 to 51 mm) river rock
- Native grasses or other perennials for banks

Arroyo (Dry Stream Bed)

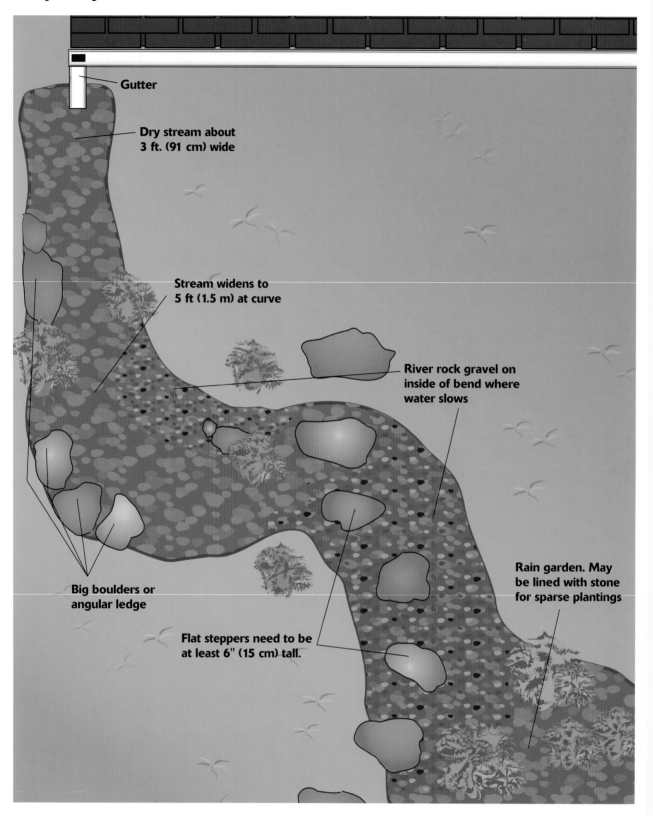

Gutter

Dry stream about 3 ft. (91 cm) wide

Stream widens to 5 ft (1.5 m) at curve

River rock gravel on inside of bend where water slows

Big boulders or angular ledge

Rain garden. May be lined with stone for sparse plantings

Flat steppers need to be at least 6" (15 cm) tall.

AN ARROYO (dry stream bed) can direct storm water to a rain garden, where flood-tolerant plants thrive.

How to Make an Arroyo

1. Call your local utilities hotline to locate buried pipes and wires. Plot the course of the streambed in landscape paint. Follow the natural course of rainwater runoff where possible. You may start the stream at some obvious source of storm water, such as a gutter or drain tile. End at a natural sink, such as a rain garden. Bends are often wider in natural streams, so make your stream wider at bends.

2. Excavate within the outline of the stream to about 12" (30 cm) deep. If you have access to a skid loader, use one for larger projects. Yard tractors also have digging accessories that can simplify the job. You can use the soil you remove to fill in low areas nearby, or to create berms and other features that work with the arroyo.

3. Rake, smooth and compact the soil within the project area. Get a bit sculptural with it. For example, you may create ledges at the edge for little rock falls. Avoid making the arroyo too uniform—vary the widths and depths.

1 Lay out the dry stream bed, following the native topography of your yard as much as possible. Mark the borders and then step back and review it from several perspectives.

2 Excavate the soil to a depth of at least 12" (30 cm) in the arroyo area. Use the soil you dig up to embellish or repair your yard.

3 Widen the arroyo in selected areas to add interest. Rake and smooth out the soil in the project area.

4 Install an underlayment of landscape fabric over the entire dry streambed. Keep the fabric loose so you have room to manipulate it later if the need arises.

5 Set larger boulders at outside bends in the arroyo. Imagine that there is a current to help you visualize where the individual stones could naturally end up.

6 Place flagstone steppers or boulders with relatively flat surfaces in a stepping stone pattern to make a pathway across the arroyo (left photo). Alternately, create a "bridge" in an area where you're likely to be walking (right photo).

If your dry stream bed comes within 10 ft. (3 m) of your house and you have water leakage problems in your basement, use two layers of 6-mil black builders plastic instead of landscape fabric near the house. This probably won't solve any problems, but it won't make them worse either.

4. Line the streambed with landscape fabric, starting from the bottom of the stream and overlapping the seams as you go up. Overlap generously and leave plenty of slack, as you might need to excavate more. Hold the fabric in place with rocks.

5. Place larger boulders along the streambed banks first; extra excavation beneath the landscape fabric may be needed to properly set extra large boulders. Strive for a natural appearance that is not too regular or uniform. Fill around large boulders and line "rapids" with smaller boulders.

6. Place flattened boulders or outcropping stones to make a stepper pathway or bridge in an area where you're likely to be walking. In most cases this feature is mostly ornamental. You may choose to build or buy a garden bridge instead. The effect can be very pleasing.

7. Fill in spaces and create gravel bottoms with river rock in the ¾" to 2" (19 to 51 cm) size range. Make sure the river rock you're using is native to your area, and avoid dumping it all into a flat field. Retain some nice shapes and contours.

8. Trim off any exposed landscape fabric. Plant native grasses and other perennials behind boulders and mulch with shredded bark. Do not use mulch where it might wash into the streambed. Plant flood-resistant plants in the rain garden (if you include one at the end of the stream bed).

7 Add more stones, including steppers and medium size landscape boulders. Use smaller aggregate to create the stream bed, filling in around, but not covering, the larger rocks.

What's a Rain Garden?

A rain garden is simply a shallow, wide depression at least ten feet away from a basement foundation that collects storm water runoff. Rain gardens are planted with native flood-tolerant plants and typically hold water for only hours after rainfall. Check your local garden center or Extension Service to find details about creating rain gardens in your area.

8 Dress up your new arroyo by planting native grasses and perennials around its banks.

Freeform Meditation Pond

If your idea of a water garden is more elaborate than most or the shape you have in mind isn't standard round or kidney, a free-form water garden with a soft, pliable pond liner may be the answer for you. And it presents yet another good opportunity to introduce stones into your landscape, both in the coping stones that surround the pond liner and as decorative specimen rocks within the pond.

Building a water garden with a soft liner is not difficult or time consuming, but the finished garden will require ongoing maintenance and care. Think carefully about your willingness and ability to provide this care before committing yourself to the project. It's also a good idea to look into local building codes—many municipalities require building permits for ponds over 18 inches (46 cm) deep. And in some municipalities you may be required to fence in the pond area so children do not have access to a drowning hazard.

Before selecting a flexible liner, compare and contrast the available types. PVC (polyvinyl chloride) liners are made from a type of synthetic vinyl that's flexible and stable as long as it does not get direct sunlight exposure. If you choose one, make sure it is not manufactured for swimming pools or roofing.

EPDM (ethylene propylene diene monomer) liners are made from a synthetic rubber that is highly flexible, extremely durable, and fish-friendly. EPDM liners remain flexible at temperatures ranging from -40 to 175°F (-40 to 79°C). They are very easy to find at building centers, garden centers and landscape supply stores, and they are also inexpensive, making them an excellent choice for DIYers. Look for a liner that's 45-mil. thick. At larger home and garden centers, you can now buy pond liner by the lineal foot.

Although some meditation ponds are not stocked, most pond owners prefer to stock them with aquatic plants at a minimum. Although goldfish and koi complicate the maintenance and often end up as snack for local predators, if you can establish a well balanced home for pond livestock you will get much satisfaction from them.

TOOLS & MATERIALS

- Level
- Shovel or spade
- Hand tamper
- Tape measure
- Garden hose or rope
- Spray paint
- Pond underlayment
- Flexible pond liner
- Sand
- Compactable gravel
- Flagstone pavers
- River rocks

How to Create a Free-form Meditation Pond

1. Select a location well away from buried utility lines. Use a garden hose or a rope to outline the pond. Avoid very sharp turns, and try for a natural looking configuration. When you're satisfied with the pond's shape, lift the hose or rope and use spray paint to mark the perimeter.

2. Find the lowest point on the perimeter and flag it for reference as the elevation benchmark. This represents the top of the pond's water-holding capacity, so all depth measurements should be taken from this point. Start digging at the deepest point (usually the middle of the pond) and work out toward the edges. For border plantings, establish one 6 to 8" (15 to 20 cm)-wide ledge about 12" (30 cm) down from the benchmark.

3. Set a level on the plant shelf to confirm that it is the same elevation throughout. Unless your building site is perfectly level or you have done a lot of earth moving, the edges of the pond are not likely to be at the same elevation, so there may be some pond liner visible between the benchmark and the high point. This can usually be concealed with plants, rocks, or by overhanging your coping more in high areas.

1 Lay out the borders of the pond by testing with a hose or rope and then outlining onto the ground with landscape marking paint.

2 Begin excavating the deepest part of the pond, which should be in the middle.

3 Excavate the plant shelf rim and check with a level.

Flexible liners adapt to nearly any shape or size pond you want. They can fit a typical kidney-shaped excavation with planting shelves, like the one shown here, or a very unique shape of your own design. EPDM rubber liner material is sold in precut sizes at your local home and garden center.

4. Dig a 4"-deep × 12"-wide (10 × 30 cm) frame around the top of the hole to make room for the coping stones (adjust the width if you are using larger stones). Remove any rocks, debris, roots, or anything sharp in the hole, and add a 2" (5 cm) layer of sand to cover the bottom.

5. Cover the bottom and sides of the excavation with pond underlayment. Pond underlayment is a shock-absorbing, woven fabric that you should be able to buy from the same source that provides your liner. If necessary, cut triangles of underlayment and fit them together, overlapping pieces as necessary to cover the contours. This is not a waterproof layer.

Tip: Call your local or state digging hotline before you begin excavating to have underground utilities plugged.

4 Dig a trench around the border for the coping stones and line it with compactable gravel.

5 Spread a sheet of pond underlayment (a bit like landscape fabric) over the excavation site to protect the rubber liner.

6 Lay the rubber liner into the excavation and use folding techniques to get it to fit the shape.

7 Begin filling the pond with water to make the liner conform to the shape of the hole. Adjust the liner as the pond fills.

8 Before filling completely, add a flat stone at the deepest part to make a base for the pond pump.

9 After the pond is full of water, lay flat coping stones around the rim of the pond to secure and conceal the liner edges.

6. Lay out the liner material and let it warm in the sun for an hour or two. Arrange the liner to cover the excavation, folding and overlapping as necessary. Place rocks around the edges to keep it from sliding into the hole.

7. Begin filling the pond with water. Watch the liner as the water level gets higher, and adjust and tuck it to minimize sharp folds and empty pockets.

8. Add some larger stones to the pond as the water rises, including a flat stone for your pond pump/filter. If the pump/filter has a fountain feature, locate it near the center. If not, locate it near the edge in an easy-to-reach spot.

9. Fill the pond all the way to the top until it overflows at the benchmark. Remove the stones holding the liner in place and begin laying flat stones, such as flagstones, around the perimeter of the pond. Cut and trim flagstones as necessary to minimize gaps.

10. Finish laying the coping stones and fill in gaps with cutoff and shards. If you are in a temperate climate, consider mortaring the coping stones, but be very careful to keep wet mortar out of the water: it kills plants and damages pump/filters. Set flagstone pavers on the ledge at the perimeter of the pond. Add more water and adjust the liner again. Fill the pond to just below the flagstones, and trim the liner.

11. Consult a garden center, an extension agent from a local university, or the Internet to help you choose plants for your pond. Include a mixture of deep-water plants, marginals, oxygenators, and floating plants. Place the plants in the pond. If necessary to bring them to the right height, set the plants on bricks or flat stones. Spread decorative gravel, sand, or mulch to cover the liner at the perimeter of the pond. Install plants along the pond's margins, if desired.

Note: Follow pump manufacturer's instructions regarding placement, wiring, and use of the filter and pump. Establish a maintenance schedule for routine and seasonal cleaning.

10 Pack small rocks around the coping stones to fill gaps and crevices. Do not use mortar—it can get into the water and kill plantlife and livestock.

11 Add marginal plantings and water plants as desired.

Resources

There is a bounty of resources to help you purchase, plan, build, grow, and develop your land. Start with your local county extension agency—an invaluable outlet for information pertaining to your land. Following is a laundry list of references for you to explore, from magazines to special-interest associations and government agencies.

Borgert Products, Inc.
Tumbled cobbles in basketweave 90 pattern (p. 131)
800-622-4952
www.borgertproducts.com

John Deere
Outdoor power equipment
309-765-8000
www.deere.com

Pave Tech, Inc.
Pave edge border edging (p. 132)
800-728-3832
www.pavetech.com

Quikrete
Joint sand (p. 133)
Cement and concrete products
800-282-5828
www.quikrete.com

Photography Credits

Alamy / www.alamy.com
p. 17 © The Garden Picture Library / Alamy (Photographer Ron Evans)

Anchor Wall Systems
p. 77 (left)

Belgard Hardscapes / www.belgard.biz
(800 899 8455 or 770 804 3363)
p. 3, 4 (top two right, lower right), 6, 8 (left), 15 (top), 16 (top), 20, 22 (all), 23 (all), 24 (lower), 27, 40, 42, 43, 126 (all)

© Crandall & Crandall
p. 79 (top left), 159 (top)

Eldorado Stone /
www.eldoradostone.com
p. 41 (all)

iStockphoto® / www.istock.com
p. 4 (top left, lower left & lower middle), 7, 8 (middle & right), 9, 10, 11 (lower), 12 (top & lower), 13, 16 (lower), 21, 24 (top), 26 (all), 28, 29 (all), 32, 78 (middle & right), 79 (left), 80, 86, 104, 110, 140, 166

John Deere / www.johndeere.com
(309 765 8000)
p. 52 (all), 53 (lower two)

© Jerry Pavia
p. 5, 15 (lower), 24 (top & lower), 25 (top & lower), 78 (left), 96, 103 (lower two), 116, 140, 154

© Susan Teare
p. 53 (top)

© Michael S. Thompson
p. 103 (top left)

Index

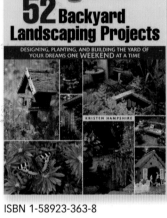